I AM I:

The In-Dweller of Your Heart

52 Inner Dictations

David Knight

DPK Publishing
1, Harringworth Road,
Gretton, Northants NN17 3DD

ISBN: 1466499354
ISBN-13: 978-1466499355

Cover art by Adeline Teh Sai Divine Inspirations.

Cover layout by Joleene Naylor

Manufactured/Produced in the United States

www.AscensionForYou.co.uk
http://AscensionForYou.wordpress.com

Also by David Knight:

Pathway
© 1998 David P. Knight
Book 1 – first published in United Kingdom in 1998 by DPK Publishing /
Redwood books.

ISBN: 09532824 06

Pathway '2nd Edition' published 11th July 2011 available as e-book on
Smashwords and Kindle:
ISBN: 978-1-4581-2756-3

Paperback on CreateSpace: ISBN 978-1463771812

Deliverance of Love, Light and Truth
© 2008 David P. Knight
Book 2 – first published in Victoria, BC, Canada in 2008 by Trafford
Publishing.

ISBN 978-142512447-2

E-Book available via Smashwords / Kindle

ISBN 978-1-4523-3728-9

For further information contact David via his blog or website:
http://AscensionForYou.wordpress.com
www.AscensionForYou.co.uk.

ACKNOWLEDGMENTS

To God, for the privilege that has been bestowed upon me so that I may receive these words of wisdom, knowledge and peace. This book has created a new stepping stone towards the eternal love and bliss that is within us all.

To all guides and teachers from within God's light hierarchy who have truly given and shared their love so freely, making my life (and heart) so rich and complete, that mere words cannot begin to describe how I feel.

I wish to thank my wife Caroline in recognition of her support, patience and love. To Adeline Teh (Sai Divine Inspirations), Robert Paskin, Elizabeth Beeton and Joleene Naylor for all their support, advice and time! To all members past and present of the Peterborough Sai Baba group and finally, thank you to my family and friends who are all so special to me.

MAY GOD BLESS YOU ALL

TABLE OF CONTENTS

52 Inner Dictations… from my Speaking Heart

Conclusion from the 'Connection'

FOREWORD

Welcome my Son. Much time in your world has passed and yet in reality no time at all.

Over the years since Book 2- Deliverance of Love, Light, and Truth was collated, we have watched and waited while your busy life has unfolded. Through many trials and tribulations both joy and happiness have prevailed. Love and Light will always shine strongly from within your heart and far beyond the four walls in which you reside.

Your understanding of whom, what, and why you exist has grown considerably over the first two books. Thoughts and feelings have emanated from your mind's eye and heart on numerous occasions regarding the subject matter and content for this new 'work'. Therefore, now is the right time David for you to collate and contribute to another book.

Since your spirituality has given you new insights, (growing brighter and lighter over time), you have realized beyond doubt that we are all 'one'. As such, shape, form, and also levels of intellect of a being, bear no resemblance to the love that is carried within and which is given so freely.

Beauty has been said to be in the 'eye' of the beholder and yet in truth, real beauty comes from the source of all things. This is God, the Creator, the Great White Spirit or whichever name or form an individual agrees within himself what pure love is.

Through the education of your Soul (in this lifetime) you have come such a long way, my Son, and yet you have not been anywhere else in time or space other than the moment that exists within each second, minute, hour, day, week or year.

There is no separation from truth and the light. There can be no doubt that for all your experiences, the happiest of all is within the 'stillness' and the bliss of love itself. So, we ask those who have picked up this new (and your third) book: where is this truth, peace and tranquility? It is in the greatest power, the brightest light, the most beautiful sight and sound and it is in you, your essence, and the very core of your existence!

Deep within your Soul and heart is the love you all seek and cherish so dearly. You do not need to travel over mountains or hide away in forests to find the answers to all things. God is everything and everything is God. As such, he dwells as the fountain of joy, cascading tears of love and peace to all who come to bathe in him.

I am I: The 'In-Dweller' of your Heart is to be the title of this latest work David. You will hear, speak, and confide in God so that many more may both comprehend and understand. Information and dictation of words will flow in a similar manner you have been accustomed to.

Others may consider that you (or we) are mad, whilst others might decree that you are indeed privileged. Your faith, hope and character have all helped in being where you are today. Listen to your heart in all that you do, for it is where you will always hear what the truth 'is'.

God knows what is to be written and when, for the benefit of society and humanity. All words and truth are simple and will be simply put. Doctrines and beliefs of many religions can often be complex but 'love and truth' is not and Spiritual education isn't either.

Sometimes you will be amazed at what is given for you to write. Some passages will make you cry with tears of peace and love. Others will make you feel that deep inside your heart there is light, glowing so brightly that people cannot fail to see and feel what is also within 'themselves'.

David, it is so good to reconnect your pen with our hearts. Know that your life is our life, and those thoughts, wishes and your dreams are felt by us too. Your earthbound time may seem to have passed by, but we have always been close, waiting patiently for you. We love you. We love you all.

Remember, the stars and planets above and beyond where we physically reside may seem an eternity away, but the mind's perception only deceives and tries to suggest this. Space, the Universe and time itself are but a minute fragment, not even the size of an atom on the Lord's foot. People say to others: 'to think outside the box', but we state that you must realize there is no 'box', so just feel and know the truth within.

May those who inquire (the aspirant or devotee) and the disciples of different races, religions and all 'beings; know that we are but one family, one Light and of one love. Connected are we all by the true source of illumination and power, the one God and one truth, the 'In-Dweller' of all our hearts.

So start to collate the written words for this new book. You will know when, for you will feel the tug of the heart. Just be still and be you. Live, breath, know and feel it. God's love and words will flow, so all you need to do is to be ready.

For now be at peace. Know that many draw close to wave goodbye. They wait in the knowing of what you will sense and feel in your tasks ahead. When it is necessary and appropriate, we'll reconnect our own 'pen' to you. From love and light within, across time, space and dimensions, good luck my son.

INTRODUCTION
From
ARCHANGEL GABRIEL

You sit as a young child, yet in truth you are not. Appearances for the many are such an important thing and the phrase, 'Beauty is only skin deep' is of course well known to you all.

Sitting eagerly to grow and patiently to know, this stillness will sustain and nourish you all and in more ways than you can often imagine. It is a replenishment of the Soul, just as a deep sleep re-energises aching limbs and muscles of the 'physical'.

Spirit works through you and is you; you are Spirit and yet why question the need for sustenance? A simple lesson would be to imagine a battery cell. If it is used, it will expel and radiate energy and as a Soul/cell of the Universal life force you are no different.

Do not envisage that you can be cut off from the power supply, for in truth you cannot. And yet, by avoidance of the true connection of yourself (both positive and negative), you then, as you have heard this very afternoon, become unbalanced. How and why is this so? Who decrees it and for what purpose? What motives lie hidden?

Nothing, dear child, is hidden. Mind's perception cannot see the truth unless true sight is born from within oneself and thy heart, which is your seat of the Soul. You see me sitting within you, opposite you and deep within your psyche, yet am I not as real as your physical?

People question (and wish) to learn and digest, but too much can be placed upon the emphasis of your natural senses. Although important, what can be neglected is your sixth sense, your intuition or 'gut-feelings' and what you feel is right from 'within'.

So, I am here and you are too. Where I am and where I go you are with me. On the Spirit realms and dimensions, distance and time have no meaning. You are Spirit and I am Spirit, and levels of understanding and growth, knowledge and wisdom, time, space and dimensions are all linked together as 'one' since 'time' immemorial.

God is love, love is god. Light is God, God is light. Spirit is God, God is Spirit and nothing is divisible or subtracted from your core essence. Your power (your light) is only diminished if you place a cloak of darkness around it yourselves. Your karma and your balance will always be yours to attain, and to also cleanse and polish your 'living' flame.

I Am I: The In-Dweller of Your Heart

Obscurity of the Soul and your memory is, and can only be, a last resort after which many, many trials and tribulations of countless lifetimes have not developed the 'inner' you. Always this is an individual Soul's choice, because you are a seed of love left to grow, but never ever left alone as you well know.

Through thick and thin your efforts to expand your light can never, ever be in vain. Your desire to learn even expands your light which is fascinating to see indeed. Positive thought creates spirals of light and truth that radiates infinitely long, but the same can be said of darkness and decay. This is why the calmness of Soul, body and mind must be one, to 'become'.

The light travels in all directions (as has been said) and also follows the same paths in reverse to your thoughts. That is why you can comprehend, "So you give and so you shall receive" and also "So you sow, so shall you reap".

Light expands Light,
Love expands Love,
Desire expands the fire.

The flame expands God's name,
The name expands the 'grain',
The 'grain' expands the same,
The same holds no blame.
Now blame can hold distain,
And distain retains the shame,
For shame can lead to blame.

The circles round again,
And 'one' you shall remain.
Until light has lead the way,
It's eternal and a day.

(Then now realise)

A shining Star is both far and near,
So search within and do not fear.
It radiates with love and light,
And our hearts are entwined all day and night.

4

I Am I: The In-Dweller of Your Heart

Know that rose coloured glasses or blurred vision,
Can erase or fade your soul's true mission.
That you and 'all' exist to grow,
To Ascend the cord that you will sow.

AMEN

JESUS...The Lord Our Teacher

With Guidance and Love to you all.

Welcome dear 'children' of love and light, that's it, sit down. All are received here for truth, love and liberty.

Know that our hearts are like the many rooms of an immeasurable house, my Father's House. If you can imagine a very large mansion, you may think that you would forget some of these rooms wouldn't you? But he doesn't, for he knows where each of his children resides, each and every minute of the day.

You might get lost or confused inside such a large place with all these different rooms, levels and floors of life. You learn and you yearn both for knowledge and wisdom yet these must come from your own experiences. Patience little ones, for as some of you know, you cannot learn any more than the level that you have reached.

Trust in love and love the trust that my Father has instilled in each and every one of you. Open your eyes, your physical eyes, and those of your mind, Soul and heart too. Then and only then, your true vision will be seen. Yes, seen more clearly, felt more dearly and understood with true love. No guilt, no pretence and no sitting on the proverbial fence.

You gather here because of love and the sharing of such far beyond these four walls. No box can contain or hide what is meant to be opened and free to flow to where it is meant to go. Hearts are entwined like the ivy that wraps around the tree. The ivy clings to the tree and wants to climb to the top, to reach the light. Likewise you also wish to climb and also reach out, for the 'tree of life' that is around and yet also within you too.

The bark of the tree enables you to grip and stay in place, so the light can reflect and radiate from within and from your face. A smile, (yes that's right), so be happy for you are all from the seed and this can be revealed by an eternal 'trace'.

Time can be so important yet it can mean nothing at all. Thousands of tomorrows, no need to beg, steal or borrow. You are all given what you need and required to experience physically, spiritually, emotionally and mentally. Some things are of course your own tests; while others are for what you can do for your fellow 'hearts' along the way. Balance is the key and your love is the door, to be opened and enable you to search for more.

Where each of you come from do not worry or concern yourselves,

6

for no matter how different you all appear to be, you are the same, yes all the same to your 'Father' and to me. Precious, like flowers and the drops of the rain which bring sustenance and nourishment but not in vain? You'll glow, radiate and spiral around, for love, true love, knows no bounds.

You'll also reach out and search both far and wide, over seas and the land and you'll look to the sky. Sometimes there'll be pain and sometimes there'll be joy and the gift of a new born child is indeed not a toy. With a chance to fulfil and to also instil, find the love from above, taking flight like a dove.

Angels and Archangels in Heaven and on Earth both look and assist the meek and the mirth. Some are below and some are above, all with their 'work' from the Lord and our God. To aid and assist you in all that you do, be glad, be safe, for He and I are in you. Go north, south, east and west, just try to do all, with love and your best. And so......

Different rooms of the house, but hearts are all safe,
For God has enveloped and surrounded you with a 'fate'.
For you are all 'from' and return unto Him,
So rejoice and all sing just like love within a hymn.

You will all grow as I have just said,
Just try to believe and rise up from your bed.
Whether morning or noon or evening or night,
The days that you walk will remain always bright.

The golden 'Son' forever glows, deep within your hearts,
Can never be extinguished or be divided into parts.
For each segment, each band, and vibration or sound,
Is eternal and as stated, true love knows no bounds.

Each day is a link and the chain keeps you all,
No 'separation and division', or an 'unearthly' fall.
So even if your life then hits a new low,
Call unto your 'Father', for he already knows.

Of what you require and of what you would all like,
To happen and 'emerge', yes from 'within' and out life.
Just 'be' and to ask with all of your heart,
For the Lord knows too, of what's right from the start.

I Am I: The In-Dweller of Your Heart

The teacher is no man or with a false text,
It is the **light** and the **love** that is 'within' that's the test.
So justify the why and then hear the call,
To know then dear 'children', you can never, ever fall.

Just be 'still'; be still… for you are the 'Divine',
And you are all 'one'… and each are all mine.
Not a possession cast aside or washed up by the tide,
For the **crown** of my **heart** I give freely, openly and will never, ever hide.

LOVE ALL…..ALL LOVE.

AMEN

LESSON 1

I AM THAT I AM

Welcome! Many of you ask, (as if seeking permission) to come into my home, my kingdom. Please know that when you have love in your heart and learn to expand and radiate this love, you will understand that you are already there!

There is no separation or division, yet it can be deemed by many that you are my children and are eternally part of me. Your core and essence too is the love that you seek and is also that of which you already give and share, but please do not ever compare.

Love is infinite and no dimension of time, space or any plane of consciousness can ever distract from this, for I am all things and of course so much more. Know that you are also all these too because you are me, as I am you. We are not apart or a 'part' of anything else, for all Creation is one and 'one' is all Creation.

There is so very much to learn and again learning is infinite, but do not ever feel that you are pressured or are running out of time. All of existence and all that you can become are to be discovered at the right moment and right place, even though you sometimes feel held back or become frustrated.

There are many virtues and traits that are deep within each and every one of you. And yet every fibre, cell and particle that forms your being is the same. You are each unique and yet, as I will always reiterate, you are also 'one'. Diverse in size, height, character and capable of different emotions and feelings maybe, but in truth with no difference at all!

Know that since time immemorial and across billions of worlds, numerous kinds of life seek answers to their questions. Deep within is where the answers lie and this is, was, and always will be so. Inside of you and in every thought and in every deed I am there, because dear child of light: I AM I.

David, I sense a query flash across your mind as you now write these words. You are concerned that some will ask, "Is this writing from a child of God? How is it possible?" The answer is simple, I am that I am….the God in me 'is'. Some will then say, "What conduit is enabling the light to pass through the mind to the hand upon a pen, and if so, how and also why and when?" This is no mystery or complex issue to discover, manipulate or

I Am I: The In-Dweller of Your Heart

bend, for you are I and I am you. Know and understand that…

My love is your love in all that I send,
for everything am I, Father, Mother or friend.
In every leaf and rock upon land, sea, and air,
you will find that my love is all and is there.

So please trust in your heart whilst learning to care,
know your hearts can be open to both feel and to share.
With your dreams and wishes and prayers that I hear,
cherished laughter and your smile… but those tears I will clear.

I recognize all hearts filled with emotions that scar,
and yet in the truth lies the door, for my heart is ajar.
Know that love taken away may indeed cause you pain,
but for those in the 'experience', it is never in vain.

And realise love does not fade like your memories can do,
for the heart retains the truth and that is in you.
My light and my love are for each and everything,
so open heart, mind and Soul to rejoice and to sing.

You will then know that deep down inside,
that I am in you and I shall not hide.

Amen.

LESSON 2

THE 'IN-DWELLER' OF THE HEART

I am you and you are me, not born or created other than through thought, word, or deed. As the many seek and grow, both within and without, there comes a time when their own realization sets in. This can be on the Earth plane or in the realm you call 'Heaven', in fact upon any of the innumerable dimensions or planes. Truth only prevails and is understood and fully grasped when it touches the very core of the self. No amount of persuasion or act of forcefulness, via body or tongue, can make someone or something truly 'understood'. It is the self, the true 'self', that knows this.

All life is moving physically, mentally, and emotionally. There, amongst this perpetual resonance lays the true stillness, yet so many can't comprehend it, but they will. When a child is given a complex sum to do they will scratch their head or perhaps even scream in frustration. When the individual embarks upon their own discovery they too can be confused, bewildered and even walk the 'path of tears' of so many souls, past, present and the future.

Perhaps you could consider this point of your lives as a test or the learning curve of the physical embodiment in which you find yourselves. Ponder and think about this when you can. For now, you can visualise a flower that blooms within your heart, the petals opening to the rays of light of the Sun. This is the truth of all things. Each petal represents facets of your 'Atma'; your Soul, your very identity.

The warmth of the Sun clears the way for the fragrance, which is your Divinity, to blossom in your being, your surroundings, in the elements and all of Creation. The energy of Love, of peace, and of Light is pure and it cannot be tainted or mislead by any known or unknown force.

On the Earth plane, scientists and philosophers of all era's past and present search in many ways for the answers to their questions. All that they could ever wish for are already within themselves. It is blindness and seeking in the dark if any other path is taken.

Do not misunderstand, human beings wish to discover and venture beyond themselves and the earth to faraway places. This is not wrong, as human endeavour can achieve so very much and within those actions of man, there can be beauty too. However, the goal is, was, and always will be to realise the truth and achieve liberation and bliss, God, Nirvana or whatever name any individual wishes to call 'ME or I'.

All must move on from the early understanding of a 'figurehead', perhaps of a statue or even of a faith, a religion and beyond. Yes, to know that you are part of me, finding the one truth – that you are me and I am you. These can be grasped and understood or cast aside as a joke or a farce. All that needs to happen is for the petals of your heart to open so the rays of Light which contain all truth will prevail and guide the seeker onto the right path. Whether you are old and grey or are an infant, you have the ability to comprehend these things if you really want to.

As you feel I feel, and it hurts me when time is wasted. I do not mean on your hobbies or individual tastes of life's choices and work. Opportunities arise in all your lives to shine like beacons of love, and yet so many go amiss. Circumstances in and around you present many openings both to give and share the beauty within each other and yet these pass by so very often.

Too much emphasis is on the material or upon selfish acts which blind, trap and twist the cords of truth that lay before and all around all things. I can see these comparisons for it is encompassed around both the individual and the masses. You can untangle yourself by letting your love bloom. Let the feelings of this fly on the wind just like pollen. Where it falls it is blessed with my grace and multiplied beyond comprehension.

Love is the nectar of my heart and I long for you all to sense its sweet taste and embrace it once more. Do not be fooled by the transient and impermanent physical world, for it is an illusion. Feel and look within yourself and discover who and what you really are and what you can become.

I know you. I know you all. There are no secrets that you can keep, no actions that go unfelt or even unheard by me while you are awake or asleep. All you do, all you think and all you are is Karma and action while in your embodiment. Break free from the cycle of physical renewal and you will be true to your Soul and goal. Wish it, want it and desire it with all that you are and can be, for it will become so.

Therefore, I see, feel and know you because I am you, the 'In-Dweller' of your heart. In both knowing and understanding this fact, you become near and dear to me. There is nothing you cannot achieve, for if it is in truth I will make it happen. Every one of you may make the one real decision and choice, of which you may need to consider. So now I ask, do you believe? I will leave your thoughts on this matter for now. You will know when to write again David. All Love, love all…..know and hear my call. Blessed be. Amen.

LESSON 3

WHO AM I?

Welcome again to the stillness and the peace, away from all the earthly things that can trouble mind and heart. It is here and only here that a true escape can be made. It is the route and direction that all must take towards fulfilment, joy and your self-realization.

As I begin this lesson today, many Souls gather around you, also to listen, learn and observe. Spiritual education, or moreover your education of your Spirit or Soul, does not cease through or from birth or death as these are merely stepping stones to aid you.

Through these cycles to erase the radiating coil of darkness and karma, many lifetimes have passed (that deep within you have all chosen for yourself). How much any individual Soul or fragment of light has grown and become lighter and brighter is also wholly dependent upon yourselves.

All are aided and guided, but as we have discussed and stated together before, 'you can lead a horse to water but you cannot make it drink'. Do not even feel slightly offended by this statement, for it is and never can be my intention for you or anyone to feel this way.

It is mentioned to reiterate that only by your own endeavours can you understand, and therefore grow in knowledge and wisdom. Remember, I am with you always and forever and therefore you are never alone. By acknowledging this you are half way there, because you will then believe in me and in yourself.

All your adversities and experiences, and also your joy and happiness will be seen as one, going hand in hand along your journey to discover and help you know who I am.

Within that sentence you could read and also sense the same expression in the question, 'Who am I?' These may appear different to the reader, the inquirer, the disciple of love and truth, but they are not.

The 'who I am and who am I?' questions are but a reflection of one truth, the inner truth, the secret, the desire and the goal for all Souls. You are me and I am you, the 'I am that I am' or God in me 'IS'. These are but a few of the countless expressions in words that try to convey and represent me in a verbal sense.

By finding the truth within yourself you will find and know me. Then you will know yourself and be able to answer the question in the title of this lesson. One may ask, is this easy? It can be what you each make it. To begin, you must find reconciliation. You need to reconcile with yourself, not by trying to change (or thinking that you can even alter) the past, but by the way you view how the past was.

It is vital that negative traits or energies are released from your heart, so that you can move forward in love and in light. Let go and do not be restrained or limited to sorrow, grief, heartache or attachment, by any situation, event or by people who come into or out of your life.

Everything you experience must be seen as an element of growth, with an ebb and flow within your life, as both a human being and as a Soul. This encourages you and will enable you to retain an unbiased viewpoint of your living in the present, erasing the trickery of the mind which tries to enforce your notion of good or bad in your experiences.

For the present to become a form of magical living, you need to firstly accept and then open your heart to the richness of peace and serenity of love that resides and is all Creation.

Ultimately you are your own teacher, educator, principal and source of Divine inspiration and guidance. If this idea is discarded, it would make the answer unknowable, even if it is right in front of you.

Therefore, I am not hidden from your view. I am not in a secret cave in a distant nation; I am not residing upon a faraway shoreline that you cannot reach. I am not hiding behind a veil of Stars in the night sky. I am not above you in a make-believe heaven, sitting upon a golden throne and I am not below you holding the earth aloft upon my shoulders and arms.

What I am is who I am,
Who am I is what I am.
This is no riddle or joke to confuse,
I do not constrain you and never abuse.

Your life and journey and the quest of your Soul,
Have tasks to complete so fulfil then your goal.
Away from the past to live in the present,
Find your true heart and love, which shines evanescent.

Karma and sin cast aside like a stone,
To return to the crown that's kept safe by my gown.
Angels and Archangels they watch every step,
So trust in your heart and not in the head.
Return to be 'still' and to rejoice in the love,
For the truth is within not below or above.

I Am I: The In-Dweller of Your Heart

When you open your heart and Soul's eyes together, you will see as one true being of light. Then, all is revealed, for no darkness or shadow can hide from the love that emanates and flows in all directions.

The illusion will be cast aside forever, so that you can nurture and also grow as the radiant spark that you truly are. Your magnificence, your beauty, your elegance and your Divinity can never again be questioned by anyone or anything.

This is what you are and have always been. It is only through the eras and passing of time that have clouded the truth, hiding it away from you and the world.

Now comes the moment to erase and finally discard the past. Like an animal or insect that sheds its skin, I urge you to reveal the new you, cleaner, brighter and more alive, stronger than ever before. There is nothing that you cannot achieve and there is nothing real that can withhold you from expressing the true love that is waiting to burst from your heart's centre.

Ignite your inner spark to become the flame of hope and joy that will carry you into eternity. Let all life see the truth within and around you. When you reveal it, then others will see me in you too.

When light emanates from you all, know that bands of golden light form rings around the earth and upon all places. Connections like links of a chain; entwined and embracing each other in friendship and peace, cannot ever be broken.

These are eternal, forged from and into my heart's fire, sealed with my grace and blessing to guide you to eternal bliss. My promise is your miracle to have and to behold and to cherish forever.

It cannot be erased, or slashed by sword or tongue,
No matter if black or white, or if you're old or young.
So whether a pale yellow or perhaps a shade of red,
Truth is beyond such trickery, of a so called fear of death.

Know you're Soul and goal, and that it will prevail,
From impermanent world see truth, right now and through a veil.
And if you are awake, or deep within a sleep,
Find the light that shines so bright, for day and night thus I do keep.
It is there that you will find, every answer that you'll seek,
From me who is the 'I', and the 'I am' that you meet.

Amen.

LESSON 4

RITUALS AND MONUMENTS

Welcome again. Ever since Souls have been incarnated onto the 'Earth plane' they have embarked upon the search for knowledge, wisdom and truth of me or 'I'.

Many millennia have passed and an untold number of people (individuals, tribes, different societies) have sought from the 'outside' world when, in fact, everything they have seen, heard, touched, smelt and tasted, as well as 'sensed,' intuitively comes from within.

When 'man' roamed through the ages, long before the stone, iron and bronze era's began, they either looked around themselves or up into the sky at night in awe and wonder and were amazed at the beauty captivating their minds and their imaginations.

Some felt that who or what they were could not be all that there was, whilst others believed that the future held only their death without consciousness and existence. In fact, these are still the viewpoints of millions of people today.

Throughout time, all sorts of deities and gods were created, not only by the masses but also by those in control, who had the power and influence over the many who would not only bend to their will but who would be too frightened to disobey or question their thoughts and actions. Many of Earth's wars and much hate has become entrenched into mind-set and heart, leading to decay, not only of the society, but of the health and well being of numerous souls.

Buildings and amazing structures would be built to honour and please that which was thought to create, save or feed life itself. Sun gods, rain gods, gods of war, and gods of love are but a few names that would reverberate and resonate in temples, circles of stone or monuments towering high into the sky.

Alternatively, tracks or scorched earth lines would pattern vast distances of land in shapes and images that could only be seen from above. They would highlight hopes and dreams of the people, wanting and waiting to receive confirmation and approval for the deeds and actions of their nation.

In your present day, billions of human beings, through their science and also faith, know so very much, and yet so many know so very little of

Truth, Love and Light. For those that do, progress could be far greater in their individual quests and journeys if what they perceive and accept in truth is actually shared and given freely without hesitation, pride, jealousy, hatred or ego.

Some require constant approval and seek illumination through complex rituals and behaviours, either in their daily activities or when contemplating me, or their life in general. Various statues, ornaments, and symbols are worshipped, as if they can actually hear the people. The attachment of such is often through need, a desire, or even a crutch to support them during difficult times.

Do not fret or feel that I am angry in any way, shape, or form, for I am not. I wish only to explain that you are me and I am you. 'Oneness' is all things, each friend, neighbour, community, country are one and whole. No division and no separation.

As such, each flower, each rock, each mountain, river, sea, and all things are me and when illusion is wiped away from the physical eyes, and the mind that plays tricks is subdued, then you can sense that all things are me. Each petal, snowflake, drop of ocean's water, tree and every animal or insect are ingredients of me.

Many cultures and civilizations have histories which depict various religious figures who have guided (or indeed misguided) individuals or the masses. I am not stating that places of worship that have spanned numerous years, should suddenly be neglected or mistreated, or that people should banish or remove what can symbolize hope and peace to many hearts. All I ask is that those who wish to pursue their Soul's path to bliss must recognise their own Divinity and not what is an impermanent figure, statue, building, or world.

Choices are of course forever your own, but when the eyes of your body, mind, and soul are seen as one, then clear vision will light up the pathway that lies before you. When this happens, you will no longer be walking in your own shadow, but rather it will be behind you forever. You will step into the light, walk in the light, and you will share in the light.

Deep within there is beauty beyond mere words. No expression, picture or image, can convey truly what you are. All of you have the potential and the power to achieve the greatest gift of all; which is self realization leading to liberation and bliss.

Who can deny you? What can deny you? It is only your self. No ritual or magic potion can relieve you of your karmic burden or your Soul's history through lives over hundreds or thousands of Earth years. What you have to do is not easy, but this can even be said of many of the everyday tasks in your life.

Though many have embarked upon multiple incarnations, some can still say, "I haven't got it right". Do not despair. Never, ever despair or fear one's actions if the heart and thoughts are pure, away from selfishness and greed or self gratification.

Let light reflect from your very being and not what can be deemed as a mirror of darkness and decay. You can succeed and you <u>will</u> succeed. Believe in yourself and simply enjoy the path that your life's road has taken you.

I will by your side; knowing, nurturing, guiding, loving and watching forever over you. Let your smile beam your joy onto others heart and let your hands do good, worthwhile actions that help and benefit others.

Do not seek greater rewards than that which you actually deserve, but feel the goodness and not ego that shines back towards you. This is a true gold that you can wear with greater value than any stone or ring that man possesses. Realise that you are rich in Spirit and much more... a Soul and Light which is brighter than a thousand Suns.

No ritual can ever be performed, or any monument built, that could match the gift of love that you share to another, both freely and truthfully. Also, as all things contain the spark and light that is I, they should be recognised as such.

In this simple fact lies the answer to all things. By acknowledging, realising and living it, your lives will become more beautiful with each passing minute.

I promise you, your dreams will come true and you will only ever shed one tear, a tear of pure joy, peace, comfort, and bliss. To try to describe a feeling of such intensity is a mistake. I love you all, as I now close this lesson with a most heartfelt and pure loving kiss. Amen.

LESSON 5

POWER OF LOVE

You are me and I am you and deep within you know it's true. So who is the King and who is the Queen? In the searching and yearning you'll know what I mean.

Far away, yet nearer than near, lies a belief but is it one of fear? You may doubt in what has been your heart's goal, a choice and a yearning for the love of your Soul.

Your light is my light, your life is my life and you're very 'all' hears my call. Illusions shattered and cast aside, while my love washes over you like an ever-flowing tide.

Cleansing and purifying is the power of my love and my grace is the tear that falls from your face. As a delicate drop of truth touched your lips, your heart aches now from my sweet embrace.

There is no division between you and of I, just like there is no difference between your senses of smell or of sight. Hearts are entwined and now fixed upon your goal, to stay within my bliss, such a cherished Soul. As Angels of Light do chant my name, in truth we are one, for we are all the same.

Now hold your thoughts yes purity of mind, all beings, all life and all of mankind. For every creature of elements, Earth, Water and in the Ether and Fire, all resonate with; from and through me never tire.

'We' are no different and the bodies they have changed, but as said before, we are really just the same. Human beings often think (or feel) they are unique, when in truth it's the self and 'I' that you seek. Yes so different by colour, creed or with your own name, but don't fooled by such a strange game.

So inspire and aspire to behold now the truth, whether you're young or old or feel long in the tooth! And be kind to those hiding behind false screens or dark curtains, for they are but veils of despair and sorrow, of that you can be certain.

Okay, your now moving away from rhythm and reason…so please know that yesterday, today and tomorrow the Sun has, and will rise, across all planes, dimensions and different places that I have created in truth, Love and Light. Know that nothing can ever truly die; everything is, was and always shall be. Do not be deluded, don't be colluded or cajoled into any other thoughts or feelings or deeds to send you from this reality. You are everything that is, was and shall be in past, present and future. For all the deception and all ills, I am the cure. Believe in me; live in me for you are me.

Understand this journey you are embracing upon is but a flicker of so called 'time'. Within me are all Light and Love and all things. Therefore your journey is my journey; your life is my life. You cannot truly die. Your bodies are your current clothes or 'house' which is very important, as it enables you to remember, experience and know me, the In-Dweller of your heart…one heart that can never part.

Be near and dear to me just as I am near and dear to you. There is nothing you can offer me other than the flower and petals of your heart's centre. All that you ever were and are now, and also what you will be, resides there. Do not be afraid, for you are cradled in my loving arms and heart. I am not your Father or Mother and you are not my child as that implies duality. There is none, for we are one and always will be.

The power of love is a Universal beacon of joy, hope and of faith in me and within you too. Its beauty is beyond compare and mankind's intellect can not yet grasp this. I am your guiding hand of Light that will help you feel your true self, the 'you and me', the 'ONE'. When 'time' is right, all will know and more importantly understand all that there is to 'become'.

The taste of your true being has washed over you tonight and the bliss you have felt lies eternal. It is everywhere, in all places and in all things. Open up the eyes of your heart to know, feel and share freely what you already possess.

For now, rest and be at peace and lay you Soul upon my breast. Feel thy heart entwined as one, thy love and Divine power beating within your chest. In Love and in Light, for now it's good 'knight'. Amen.

LESSON 6

STILLNESS

When you become 'still', you feel the love that is both you and I flowing through, to, and from all things. Like the blood that flows through your body and veins, I am the life force that enables you to do all the activities of your Soul, helping you to accomplish all that your heart needs to. My breath is the life force and energy of creation and I am here for all life, all 'beings', and for all time.

If I am you and you are me, then we are one. We cannot be divided, separated or broken. We are whole, everything, nothing less and nothing more. This is most felt and understood when you are at your most peaceful and still. By focusing on the inner you, you are focusing on me and then the feeling of realization and self- realization takes place.

In understanding this you will fulfil your goal, your one true goal and dream…into immortality of bliss and perfection, an embrace of pure Love and Light that will captivate and enthral you, nothing else will or can compare. Everything else is pretence, false and impermanent, which so many believe is the truth when it is not. So to, no one can help another fulfil their own goal, for each and everyone have their own part to play, their own karma (body and action) to unfold.

By becoming 'still', an opening arises for each Soul. It is like a doorway through and into darkness emerging into light. Journeys such as this must be taken so understanding, knowledge, experience and enlightenment can follow. Someone who has the patience and forbearance to continue will know no bounds. The only limit is placed upon oneself, by your own heart.

When you contemplate and are within pure stillness, everything resonates in time together. Your vibration / energy, light and love connect with me. By being still you receive and also send power, returning it back to me. Energy spirals like a beautiful rainbow across time and space, a marvel to see and comprehend. Love beaming, yet also fragmenting into sparks of an eternal flame from a fire burning within me.

As you sit and wonder, sometimes contemplating all that there is around you, it is the beauty 'within' that is forgotten, pushed aside until another day, week, month, or year. Time waits for no man, an ever lasting river that carries you along, but not to where you truly belong, which is to and with me eternally. I wait, I wait, and I wait. I am your shoreline and

21

your rescue. You do not need to send an SOS for I am already here, within you. It is only the recognition of this that helps lead you to your eternal future.

Hear me. Hear my voice in the daytime, at night time and while you're asleep. One voice is all that you need to recognise within the darkness of the impermanent world. My voice is the light, the only light that you can hear and see in eternal truth. When you become still you will know implicitly and simply that these things are true, nothing else and nothing more.

I have said to you before that when you are truly 'still' a thousand bells could chime but you would not hear them, instead only me, you and the truth. But, what does one expect? What beauty, what awe-inspiring scene would be sensed by sight, smell, touch, taste, or by hearing it?

Know that I am the warmth if you were cold. I am the drink that would quench your thirst. I am the light when you are blinded by darkness. I am the land that encircles the ocean of doubt. I am the sky and clouds that drift by watching over you. I am the mountain that you climb in earnest and will eventually reach the peak, standing alone, yet entwined within my heart you'll be. I am the fragrance of sweetness from a flower. I am the air that fills your lungs and I am the touch that caresses your face in a loving embrace. I am everything and everything I am.

Understand this too, that you and I are one and as such you are God. It is fact not fiction. I am the in-Dweller of your heart and we never part. Your body and all bodies are but golden chariots that carry you upon your journey. Focus then on the 'innerness' of you, but do not neglect both who and what your chariot is and does.

If you're a human being, act like one that is true to each and everything else that resides with and around you. Do not succumb to lower senses, but rise above negative energies and situations that can ensnare and encircle those who are unprepared. There is absolutely nothing that you cannot achieve if you have faith in yourself. As spoken before, if you have faith in yourself then you have faith in me. Love yourself and love your 'self' (the inner you) and accomplish your destiny.

Do not remain deep seated, deep rooted and struggling, but start to spread your wing of love and light, taking flight into the well of your heart. This 'well' is the key to all things and, as it is eternal, you will forever fly with me as I am your other wing to joy and peace.

Do not fear anything while embracing new opportunities that feel right (within you) in your life. In your difficult times I will support, carry and help you all I can. If you are in pain, for whatever reason, think of and focus on me. In your so called happy times of laughter and joy, I will watch you and laugh and feel the joy with you. I am the answer to all your questions, all your queries and all the missing pieces of your life's jigsaw. When you see me, feel me, and know me, the 'picture' will be complete. No more returning of birth and death. No more yearning or despairing. You will not want for anything, for nothing else will be desired or required ever again.

So be silent, turn within and find your self and me. I am waiting, waiting always for you. I will never leave you for I cannot leave myself. Be 'still'. Know it, want it, wish and pray for it. Remember; be near and dear for without exception, I am Love and Light, always and forever. Amen.

LESSON 7

ENERGY

As your heart wells up with feelings of love, I know of the grieving that has beset you and Caroline during this week. I also know you sense me with more than just your body. As your tears fall, I feel them. As you ache inside, I will not hide. I will lift you up with my grace and my blessings to new heights. I will bring smiles back to your faces that will shine like beacons to those who draw close from far and wide. Do not be sad, for she (Daisy) is with me, in my heart and my kingdom that encompasses all things. Do not suffer with pangs of guilt for which you both are clear.

All people should know that sometimes dreams and wishes become their own nightmare. It is down to perception and fear, a fear that they have no control over their destiny. This is strange when all it takes is belief and faith in oneself, the faith that is me. Life isn't always about fairy tales and happy endings, but these should not be taken for granted of course when they come true.

Life is your body, your karma, your right action, and experiences that come to you, and situations that get played out before, with and by you, do so for your growth. These occurrences, or you could say these energies, are all around you as different vibrations, different levels of ether, matter, and emotions of your 'being'.

During your life stages of rebirth, education, employment, retirement, and old age, many different types of energy will come into and around you. You cannot dissect, burn, erase, or hide from it. Energy is life and all life derives from it. You could take this a step further and call energy 'Love'. How so? How can you touch love, feel love or know love? Well, in a simple analogy, name me one person who has not cried, laughed or shouted out aloud. Does an innate object do these things? No. It is this simple.

As I am love and energy, I am all things in all places, dimensions and encompass all time. There is nothing that I do not sense or cannot feel. This is why I feel pain and anguish as readily as your joy. People often ask me, "Why have you not intervened? Why did you let this happen?" In grief and pain of heart things are said with anger, hatred and desperation.

Through understanding and knowledge you will find truth. In finding truth you will come full circle to peace and to know true love. All must focus on who and what they are and the energy of who you are, what you think and what you say. All deeds, thoughts and actions are energy and this can be either positive or negative, resulting in the appropriate outcome of helping, protecting, nurturing and loving, or the complete opposite could occur.

As you sit, you think of the body which was born, a birth of energy. In fact, your physical is the only thing that was born as your essence, your Atma; your Soul was never 'born' into the physical world. You already existed; for you are permanent and what is permanent cannot die. Only the impermanent fades and dies.

When you look into the night sky on a clear evening and see the multitude of stars, (so many that man can't really perceive), these are being born and fade all the time. When stars collapse and become black holes a change of energy has taken place, it has altered, yet still exists.

A human being goes through similar processes; evolving, growing, maturing, but, as the body is born, it follows that it will die. This 'body' is cremated or buried, perhaps in time it is either transmuted into another form by fire and ash or dissolved into earth. Everything is returned to me, as I am all things.

Those who do not know me in their hearts, I still love. Everyone is near and dear to me, and the realization of such, one day, will happen. All will sail on my ocean of love, for I am the wind that will empower those that flounder by the rocks. I will remove the anchor (or you could say 'anger'), that weighs them down in the false position of a make-believe harbour within the physical world, with its materialism and traits of ego, personified by lack of compassion and mistrust.

This harbour that pretends to be a safe haven from the elements is in fact (for many) a prison. Who says that they cannot or mustn't venture outside? Why is one frightened to experience the new horizon? The so called sanctuary is the illusion of people's minds and hearts. A false energy, a harness holding one down when you could be breaking free to eternal bliss, to me.

For one to progress, just take a step towards me. For one to achieve what they think is impossible, take three. Push aside the clouds of doubt and enter my heart that is yours, for it always was and always will be. I am you and you are me. We are 'one' energy, but sometimes in your confusion you feel as if we are separate, running parallel to each other.

Know that I truly love you and our hearts are one. Every heart beat that resonates around the physical world I know, I hear and I feel you. Be still. Feel the energy 'within and out'. Do not ever despair, for nothing and no one is alone, I will always care. Remember, 'she' is safe in my hands, no suffering, no fear, just peace and bliss. Be 'still' and feel me, like I feel you. Amen.

LESSON 8

GRIEF, 'HEART-ACHE' AND THEN JOY

Welcome. As you write the title of this passage, you may immediately think that there is a particular sequence of events that occurs. Obviously, from past experiences, you know that this is not always the case but true joy is forever and it is forever within you too.

Nothing, no one, or any 'being' needs to feel pain and anguish before they know joy, however it is the very nature of your mind and way of living that trick you to believe that this is so.

I have watched and felt your emotional rollercoaster of recent days. Jasper, your beloved cat who had been suffering from old age and illness would never have lived, even to recent times, without Caroline's and your love washing over him during years of togetherness.

As your tears flowed and your hearts ached in distress as he slipped away, Angels and guardians who watch over all animals and creatures escorted and carried him to peace and contentment within my light that radiates for all beings. Know that he is amongst his friends and with those on the ethereal planes of vibration who know you both. They are caring for him, so he is fine and free from pain and anguish. He will be waiting for you when you yourselves are ready to Ascend and cross into your permanent state.

'Pud', as you often called him, lived on the earth plane until he was meant to leave. In the time when you're grieving is most apparent, your mind tricks you. All people who feel that they lose their loved one - a relative, a friend, or pet - feel this trickery.

By now you have the experience to deal with such things as the knowledge has turned to wisdom. The love, light and acceptance of these events should now allow you to be unshaken by this or other difficult circumstances. Some may feel that it is harsh of me to suggest that you need to overcome burdens such as these more easily, but this is what I am now asking you to do.

I will never ever, ever ask you to abandon your feelings of oneness and love for another person, being, or a beloved pet. What you should continually strive to achieve is the release of your attachment. These are not the same thing. How can the devotee, aspirant, disciple, or the person looking for answers define it simply and clearly? The key is within yourselves and all it takes is recognition and remembering who and what you are, as we have described many times before.

It can be very easy to be deceived at times of stress and struggle, but these are precisely the events and occasions when your inner strength needs to prevail and let go of negativity. Accept that events are as they should be in terms of karma and right action. The struggle is to overcome feeling separate. One feels and thinks that they are divided. This is my husband, my wife, my child, or my pet. In truth they are not, for they are all you and me. All are 'one'.

Some feel that their 'God' presides over them or lives in a particular place, or they may gaze upon a statue or alter which depicts in their eyes who or what I am. As stated, there is no separation so then I am all things and all things are me. I am the flower that is wilting and I am the next flower that blooms. I am the tree with no leaves and I am the tree whose blossom flies in the wind. I am the desert and the seas and I am the above and below.

As such, no one or 'nothing' can be alone, even in your darkest hour or the happiest moment of your life. So, if you now understand this and an event that you call 'death' occurs close to you, by concluding that the attachment is false, then there is no loss. If there is no loss then there is no fear. No fear means that there is no anguish or grief. Without grief you will not shed tears of pain, but rather tears of joy and celebration of a life that has enriched you and all those who come to know them.

This connection cannot be erased. Memory or even time can fade what was once so strong, but the love that is contained within two hearts cannot be destroyed by anyone or anything. Fire, water, earth or sky cannot burn, erode, bury, or be elevated away. As the love was held by both hearts it cannot be extinguished, then there is no need to cry, no matter what the circumstances and events have conspired and bought to bear.

All egos must be diluted, so false thoughts cannot interfere with the process of truth. Yes, the truth is that the heart and Soul cannot 'perish' by any man-made event. People sometimes conclude that acts of violence by so called madmen mean that they have no heart and Soul. Know that even a 'madman' (a perception made on earth) loves something or someone. I explain this because it is often so difficult for you to comprehend or explain why and how a human being could inflict pain or harm upon another.

Causes and triggers, such as pride, hate, anger, and jealousy burn deep within the psyche. They lurk and hide within the shadows and recesses of the mind and body, looking for ways to express themselves. Instead, love and compassion, kindness and forgiveness need to grow within the heart. These seeds of truth can multiply and expand, touching and reaching far beyond boundaries of imagined walls; physically, mentally and emotionally. So, live with dignity and with values that have enabled you to be called a human being.

You are all so special, so strive to do and be the best person that you can be. Any job or activities that you engage in are all by-products and these, if undertaken in truth and love, are for the well-being of your fellow-man and for society.

All acts of kindness reverberate like the chimes of a bell for they echo and expand upon waves of love and light. Your hearts do not need to bear hurt and fear and they do not need to cry out for tears to fall in pain. Do not miss or despair when ' letting go' of someone (or a pet), but continue to rejoice and sing their name in praise, for having the wonderful opportunity and time you had together on the plane of existence you currently reside upon. Please know that as 'one' I shall be:

-The boat that carries you across the ocean(s) of your emotions.

-The land you walk upon holding you upright and true.

-The wind that blows away dark clouds from your body, mind and Soul.

-The spiritual 'vision' to reveal the light and the Sun to radiate warmth and love in your heart.

-The hand that lifts you up from the ground when you feel you can't go on.

-The life giving 'water' that will quench your thirst for truth, knowledge and for wisdom.

-The spark deep within that gives you everlasting life.

-The colours of the rainbow shining down upon your darkened days of false fear and tears.

We are **one** forever. Please do not grieve. Erase the heartache and pain. You are joy itself so live, breath, know and understand it. Love conquers all things that you can ever possibly imagine to fear. So do not, as you are nearer than near to me. I love you all. Amen.

LESSON 9

JOY OUT OF DARKNESS

The depths of the darkness, the night, the deep, hatred, or the abyss, are all names of the so called 'negativity' and fear. However, from them all know that there is and always will be the 'positive' and light. This is called balance. In all walks of life, within and upon all planets, dimensions of time and space, and in all vibrations this is so.

In your deepest, darkest hour there is always a glimmer, a faint speck of light, joy, and hope. This can never ever be erased by any human being, creature or energy vibration. For nothing can destroy true light and love.

Much has been said or written on these facts before, often in text that is confusing, over-elaborated or even symbolic in nature. Simplicity is the **key** to truth, knowledge, and wisdom and a 'heart' is the **lock.** Once combined, these reveal true insight, an insight into my love.

As your musical notes flow around the room in which you sit, they fill the energy with a rate of vibration that's pure gold. These are not material or transient to the physical, but are soft flowing rhythms of majestic notes that ride in waves of peace and joy to all that gather and hear it within themselves. No magical tricks or disguised, bewildered looks of expression are here.

It is clear that sometimes when the Soul seems lost or confused and almost at the point of giving up, there is a spark to be found. So then, know that at this Easter time, a special reflection of your faith mirrors in many a heart's flame.

When the Lord Jesus was crucified and the heavens went black, many believed the world was coming to an end and questioned, "How could the Saviour die? How did he not save himself? Why did God not save his Son?"

On the third day Jesus was raised in body, spirit, and Soul and thus joy came from darkness. He endured the most painful experience, not just from the cross but within his heart by the people, his 'family' whom he had come to guide and lead to me. His experience was necessary and ordained by me, acted out by destiny and fate to lead you from the darkness into light.

Those with karma, known or unknown to them, have only to enter their true heart to find him, for the Lord sits at the seat of each and every Soul. He is part of the eternal flame of golden love so bright and so magnificent that his light emanates and permeates in all directions.

I Am I: The In-Dweller of Your Heart

It flows just like a gentle stream washing and wearing away the rocks of your sin that you yourselves have created. His true love can gradually erode the rock or can instantly make it vanish for it knows no bounds and can conquer all fears and ills; it is pure joy.

Often karma is like granite because of the depths of the darkness that resides there. Also, many lifetimes can be undertaken for it to be worn away by the bearer. This is due to the fact that numerous lessons must be learnt through themselves or is for those that they live, meet, work with, or even strangers just passing by in the blink of an eye.

Over time though, even granite erodes into dust, just like your physical bodies, until they and 'you' are balanced in all senses of the word. However, even dust leaves a trace and so does the memory of your lifetime, journey, and legacy.

This Easter, there is an inheritance to be rediscovered by many Souls. It is a reconnection to the joy that has been given to 'all' in times of their deepest, darkest hours. All that is required is an open heart, free will, compassion, and forgiveness. Is this too much? No, for these things are all and in everything. They only have to be acted upon once they have been recognised within oneself.

Therein lies the choices to be made and these are clear upon the Soul. The Lord upon the cross did not falter upon his quest, goal, and life's work to bring my love, vision, insight, and light to you all. It is in recognising Jesus' light and love upon the cross that you therein discover your own: one light and one love in all, from all to all.

Once known, it is the choice of the individual to discount and deny, or to embrace and accept, who, what, and also the why that you 'are'. Understand that when the Sun shines upon your face you feel uplifted, but when it shines upon your heart you feel complete, even though you already actually are!

Imagine the joy of a lost child then embraced by distraught parents, a stranded person airlifted to safety, or the discovery that you're beloved is alive and well. Even these and so many more like them, are just fragments of joy compared to the feeling of oneness, the magnificent love and light.

You will eventually cross over into the permanence of me which is your 'homecoming' after you life's work, karma, and destiny have been cast and fulfilled. Remember though, this is not a game or a roll of the dice, but eternally entered voluntarily and willingly by all Souls.

You have all required 'time' to become what you have become and to do what you need to do. Use whatever you have wished for and have required in being the best human being you can be. Release your never-ending supply of my love for truth, honesty, compassion, and forgiveness.

Be what you all were, are and always will be and that is a fragment of my expression, peace and joy out of the darkness!

A SOUL'S GOAL

You strive to be 'one' yet you're already free,
And your Soul is a branch or a leaf on the tree.
To then float on the breeze and be taken by free-will,
Know sometimes you'll struggle to climb up life's hill.

You journey alone, yet you're never apart,
A connection is in truth if the heart is ajar.
Like a door so strong, made of fine spiritual oak,
Enter in and be bathed by my joy; lie and soak.

Emerge and sustain in your new zest for life,
Be gentle and kind; love your friend, husband or wife.
Walk the good walk and talk the good talk,
And be true to your Soul to fulfil your true 'goal'.

Amen.

LESSON 10

THE 'GOAL'

Welcome to one and all. We have looked at small segments, or rather small pieces of information so far that briefly describe the purpose of your Earth-bound existence. Moreover, I have reiterated various reasons for your current embodiment which is due to your karmic (action) 'imbalance'.

I explained these to help quench your continuing thirst for wisdom and self-knowledge upon the road that you are taking at this time of your lives. People go from day to day and year to year, without ever venturing past minor doubts or misapprehensions.

That said, even a small step to self-realization is better than none. For those who deny I exist, then it can be said or described as them having distanced themselves too far away from me in their mind or thoughts. This is only because deep within their true heart, as for all Souls, you would recognise me instantly.

I do not chastise anyone, no matter whom or whatever they become or choose to be. The important issue, as with any situation or event, is whether it is said or done with truth and honesty. These are the issues that make up your true character and this is the net result of your thoughts, words, and deeds.

If someone truly denies that Love and Light exist, then they are in fact becoming 'zombie' like; living in shadow, hiding, and pretending that they can see in the dark. In these examples, the only light and love that can be seen or felt is from within 'oneself'. A 'spiritual' magnifying glass or microscope would be needed to 'focus' on what is their core flame, sadly dimmed, but still effulgent with beauty and elegance beyond compare.

None the less, you all have choices to make, even on a minute by minute basis to do what's right. Some will say, "But what is the right thing to do in such a fast-paced and sometimes disturbing world in which we live?" Always the answer is simple and I will simply put it across to you in rhyme and reason.

Right or wrong are words in a song,
And truth is the way from youth to old age.
So do what you feel and feel what you do,
But know tears that fall are from 'one' not two.

Discuss, meditate or just let these words wash over you. All life (and your life) can be as simple or as complicated as you make it.

In whatever circumstances you find yourselves in, try to be content. I do not mean that you should not strive to achieve your aims and wishes but rather be satisfied with who and what you are in all areas of mind, body and Soul. These may seem separate yet are whole, as each have an important impact and effect on each other.

The mind can be a true friend or can lead you up the 'garden path' to illusion and the confusion that we have discussed many times before. Do you let your senses control you - or do you control your senses? Your thoughts often betray you and disguise the truth that is but a breath or heartbeat away.

In realising this, you can put into place positive processes to quell your sensual desires and of what you 'think' you want and need. Being positive helps breed greater sources of information and guidance to reach those who firstly reach out for themselves. Help and love is there for all if the body, Soul and mind work in unison to truly 'see' it.

Understand that the body is impermanent and is dying the moment the physical is 'reborn'. This is why it is important to look after it, for it will aid and help you to achieve so much in your lives. Do not ever think that if your body is not what others call 'complete'...that you're any less a person or (in truth), a being of light and love in the eyes of my heart.

Everyone is whole to me and your history and karma playing out has no bearing in whether you deserve to achieve your goal or not. That said, people can do crazy things for crazy reasons and again, you must be accountable for the choices that are made at any point in your life.

Regarding the Soul, a long time ago it was written that on a Soul level those that were evil would always be held accountable and that as punishment they could lose their 'Souls memories'. If I were to say to you I could not do such things, would some think me weak or unable to intervene in any way shape or form? Right now though, try to think about this on a lesser scale. For instance, such as a teacher who controls their pupils with detention or if a parent berates their child for misdemeanours carried out.

First and foremost understand that I am 'pure' love and light and so freewill was granted not by any governing power other than that of whom and what you (and me) already are. For this reason, all your reaction to action, your cause to the effect can be nothing more than this.

So in fact, your Soul shines as bright as a billion suns or as a dim light being covered by a blanket of hate and doubt. To remove such impediments simply tug or pull them away as quickly as you can, just as if you were removing a thorn from your foot or finger. Relief from anguish and pain will be instantaneous, as if morphine had been administered to you.

Then, in turn, your life will become free of false desires that bind and hold you within the pretence of embodiment. Your self-realization and your goal ahead will be lit, a shining glory that you can wear like a crown, majestic and brilliant reflecting within and without all the love you truly behold.

The 'goal' as I have stated is always sought 'within'. First and foremost it is the only way. You will not find it in any other human being, as every embodiment, no matter how loving, how peaceful, or how beautiful, has their own karma to balance and their own life and road to follow.

All books and literature of any religious persuasion can only assist as guides and they should help you to realise that you need to discover the reality yourself. No one or any 'thing' should ever insist that you hurt any other being. Remember, so you sow so shall you reap! If not on this 'earth plane,' then karma will always play its part in truth in all dimensions and vibration levels that exist.

To reach fulfilment, bliss and peace in me is your only 'goal' which circumnavigates across every sinew of your being. It is inherent within you all, even if no sign of this choice or search is shining on the exterior 'you'. It is a spiritual link, finer and far more complex than any scientist's equation or DNA sequence. With this considered, it is still simpler and much easier than a child's 'ABC'.

Ignore fear and understand you are simply love. Yes; to love, from love, by love, in love, and all love. If you deny yourself then you are also denying me. Accepting yourself is accepting me in your heart, Soul, and mind, and in all things. Truly, this is the simplest explanation of them all. Amen.

LESSON 11

THREE

Within the silence, thoughts and feelings now emerge. Are these from the mind, the heart or from both? Perhaps they are even transmuted and connected by another 'form' or even released from deep within your Soul.

In this extract I will explain and let you digest what I mean regarding these things and of the title of this lesson too. Many people, who will read this and then contemplate upon it, will discover a deeper understanding of what is involved and the process to which they need to strive and pursue to reach their true 'goal'.

When someone thinks of the word 'three' it could conjure up the straightforward numerical number or a much deeper expanding thought. This could range from simple numerology to the power of three encompassing Mind, Body, Spirit; the Father, Son and Holy Ghost; or even Faith, Hope and Charity. Often these elements are stated and digested within one's thought process as the holy trinity. Today I am going to ask you to put any preconceptions to one side and for you to simply think of 'three' as the following – Man, Beast and God.

In your daily endeavours many situations arise. This ranges from the rituals of working, eating, and sleeping as well as your thoughts, words, and deeds that you engage in subconsciously and consciously. In all these there are choices and decisions to make. Within them all your thoughts and actions take one of the aforementioned three that I have stated. Are your desires, hopes and dreams controlled by one or by all three?

When you kindly help another living thing what has taken place? When hurtful actions, words or thoughts have manifested themselves far beyond your four walls, are they human, Godly or of a beastly trait? As you read you need to understand and place what is being imprinted upon your mind regarding your daily situations, then contemplate on the direct result. Or, just simply let the 'impression' of such drip through to your consciousness and also upon your heart.

Are the feelings and thoughts of 'desire' (whether they are material, mental or physical) degrading the resulting actions you take? Does the 'desire' in its varying forms make you feel different in any way? Do they, upon analysis, show that they are lowering your vibration and energy of your Soul? Some would say they do as one can become animalistic, 'beastly' and 'un-Godly'.

If you could choose the resulting consequence of all your actions, thoughts and deeds, then there you must only strive for one eventuality and that it should be 'Godly'. People will say that this is easier said than done. Of course it is.

The inquirer, the aspirant, or the devotee must always consider the result and of which of the 'three' will prevail. In reality, for every Soul to reach the goal of eternal bliss in me then 'Godly' must be the number one, the winner and the master of all things. Do not waver or believe that you will not win. Think of things as a race but some will give up while some will get side tracked taking what they believe are easier roads, when in fact there are none.

How long does it take to win? Did the Tortoise not beat the Hare in the tale and fable? Some of you will find the path you are taking is short, for others it will take their whole lifetime. One should not be equated as better than the other though, as each individual has their own karma to balance and work through. (Remember do not judge; lest ye be judged). Do not be concerned over 'time' in terms of days, weeks, months or years, as I have explained before, it waits for no man. Comprehend that I am the shoreline and your harbour and it is within me that you will find eternal rest and peace.

Know that as each morning breaks and the Sun rises in the phenomenal world, the light brings warmth and substance to all living things. In the same way the illumination of your heart and Soul radiates and reflects all that you have been, are and will be. Likewise, your whole being can reveal these in the form of Human, Beastly or Godly actions and qualities.

This is very important for as each individual grows and matures the 'three' elements will be expressed through your character, personality and attitudes in everything that comes into contact with you. Moreover, a person, a situation or even an environment will also cause you to think and react in one of the ways described.

Deep down you have the choice and 'within' you are me and I am you. Therefore, it is remembering, and then experiencing truth in your search through your daily life that will dictate the outcome. In each of you, your Divinity holds no doubts and holds no blame or shame. It is the wrapping (your body plus the illusion and confusion) which hides this, concealing the beauty and the peace, because it deludes, cajoles, and even despises.

At Christmas time or a birthday, everyone despises, wants, or needs something and it is usually in the material sense. Therefore, please picture a scene of a child ripping open a gift, the wrapping being cast fervently aside in the eagerness to see the 'prize' inside. In essence, everyone should be like that, but with desperation and a yearning for the hidden gift of Love, Light and Truth 'within' instead.

Some may say that a child, in its readiness to reveal and know what is contained by the paper, does not even take time to know who the gift is from. Parents or next of kin may even feel annoyed or anguished at this, citing that their child's sheer excitement got the better of them.

Well, know that I too wish you all to have joy in unveiling what you so desperately seek and need. The outer 'wrapping' over the gift inside (which is the true you) is not permanent and so is cast aside, buried or burnt. Know that I am not concerned with all that envelopes your truth within, for your looks, appearance, and material wealth are all by-products and are not permanent and sustainable.

Upon physical birth and embodiment you have nothing and you return with nothing. Only the essence of your Soul and being remain intact, though your karma (right action) will have played its part, balancing, erasing, or even multiplying.

In the example of the child and its gift, I said that upon opening it they did not wait to see who the gift was from. Well, the gift of true love that is you does not need and cannot be 'labelled'. It needs no 'tag' to express a 'to' and 'from' as love is, was and always will be.

It is in all Creation and it is truly you and I. It is this fact above all things that makes you 'Godly' and because of this; it is the element of the 'three' that will live forever more. In peace and blessings live your today. You are the 'present' (pre-sent) and my 'gift', for we are all 'one'. Amen.

LESSON 12

A CHRISTMAS CAROL

As you sit you can feel the pressure in and around your head, could this be communication from the so called 'dead'? As you become 'still', many other souls draw close to you, from all walks of life and existence. This is because they can grow, learn and digest truth and meaning too. Not only do they hear and see, but they feel the information and the love that is given and sent 'within' and 'out'.

Often people think they are alone, this cannot be so as I keep reiterating to you. I shall always remind you of this until it is etched firmly within all aspects of your being. When one experiences natural or so called unnatural phenomena, the receiver or practitioner will sense numerous different feelings and also come to many different conclusions.

When something feels correct for the individual (or for those that hear, sense, view, and are nearby) then a resonance, a spark, a true feeling of joy and fulfilment occurs within the heart. It is through these experiences that I help you on your journey, quest and only true desire to become permanently with me in all aspects of your being.

With these coming festivities, I hope the masses celebrate with open hearts; sharing the love within, sowing seeds of truth that can grow fruitfully and can be harvested at a later date when required to do so.

Those with Christian beliefs will probably have a Christmas tree. These trees, whether real or artificial, will be adorned with decorations and the like. In reality this is but a reflection of the truth. A real pine tree with its pine needles, (which can be soft and gentle or hard and sharp) bears so much more.

A tree such as this has a wonderful shape and its aura of luminosity as it lives is something to behold. You can sense its light like a star which manifests from all points and radiates in all directions. It is both beautiful and serene, created by and from love.

I explain this to you (and it is so reticent) because although many bring such stresses and strains upon oneself due to commercial, materialistic, and family pressures, it is only when you start to relax and actually be at peace that the same light and ambience as the pine tree then manifests itself to touch those around you.

Please understand then that happiness, joy, peace, goodwill, friendship, forgiveness, and compassion for another soul or being are all magnified and personified when truth flourishes from the heart, especially now.

So, when in this special atmosphere of love and light, be like the pine tree's branches and extend your arms and heart to another. Let it touch a broken heart; let your light be a beacon when those who have cast aside their doubt go looking for guidance. Comprehend that nurture and nature go hand in hand. So many aspects of a human being's life are like this and in time all will understand who and what they are.

As Christmas approaches many will gather in the name of the Lord and sing praises of 'God's love'. People will come together for many different reasons, but all will be touched in some way by the uplifting hymns and carols. Often it is the words that bring meaning to one person but for another, it could be the 'sensing of' or a heightened awareness of much more than this.

Indeed, over the millennia and eras of time, souls have gathered in worship and prayer to many a so called 'God'. Civilisations since time immemorial have believed in one form or another. They have felt that there was always something greater than themselves. As I am all things and all Creation is me (as you all are), then all along they have just been recognising what was inside of them.

If one should bear witness to scenes, images or actual events (such as a solar eclipse), though they are but physical and impermanent, this does not matter. It is in the sensing and in feeling that the soul receives the key. It is a key to the remembrance and experience in whatever way makes sense to the individual, or masses, of me. Remember, I am love and love is all things.

Tonight will be shorter for you in terms of the 'understanding' shared and known. I pause in liaising with you at this time, for you to reflect on a Christmas feeling, a prayer or carol. Let the reader decide what part it plays in their hearts.

A Christmas Carol

Two hearts that beat as one,
Louder and louder they do become.
Linked in truth and by hand in hand,
Travel through time to the Promised Land.

I Am I: The In-Dweller of Your Heart

Souls drift by in search of the Son,
They pass through the love of the enlightened 'one'.
Knowledge and understanding given freely to all,
Open hearts and arms wide when you hear the call.

Time waits for no man, or beast, or being,
And I am the truth, all perceiving and all seeing.
All you have to do is to become the one,
Your immortality, the bliss in truth you'll have won.

Your goal has been set and is the path you now take,
Past lives and your history are not what are at stake.
It's the present you're given, like under the tree,
Find victory not defeat and forever be in me.

One Love and Light that encompasses all things,
Not manufactured by hands or made by machines.
The ingredients of your body and of the 'physical' world,
Always to be erased, just like I said and have told.

So then go forth, with a spring in your step,
Renew your 'own' faith no matter what you 'get'.
As long as you hold, true love in your heart,
It doesn't matter which, for we will never ever part.

Peace, love and blessings to you all,
Amen.

LESSON 13

PEACE AND GOODWILL

Welcome again. Love and Light flows to all who gather and draw near to me. Peace and goodwill too, or is it so called 'God's' will? Each and every day you use your God-given freewill to embark upon your thoughts, words and deeds, but are these freewill or the will of the Divinity within you which enables you to shine more brightly, offering peace and balance to those whom you meet?

Do not think that relationships, acquaintances, or meetings of like minds happen by chance. You are guided to go where you are needed most, for both others and your own experiences. Consider this not as fate but the pathway to greater things. Understand that destiny, nirvana, and bliss are just ways to describe the goal for each and every Soul.

Know too that when words are spoken softly they can uplift many a heart, or, when said in anger or with hate, they can cut down like a sword the very Soul which is a reflection of your own and is also me. See the Divinity in all and you will see yourself and your true 'self'.

When you assist in these various ways, spirals of love and light energy swirl outwardly and above thee, like a DNA helix touching and melting within the vibration energy all around Creation. These spirals can travel through all dimensions, through time and space far beyond your phenomenal world and earth plane. When love and light comes from a true heart, nothing can erase it or break it in to two. It is all pervading.

On the earth plane many are preparing for your Christmas time, which is a season for peace and goodwill. As mentioned before, this can be a worrying period for lots of reasons, especially to those hearts that radiate with despair, anger or hate. A helping hand is all that is needed in most situations. This outstretched hand could be in forgiveness, compassion, or to give strength and hope to another. In whatever form, this help is the spark that ignites the peace to flourish within a heart.

If assistance is given in truth, then the recipient benefits, but so do all those who gather and witness such an event. This is because indirectly the kindness is magnified in the aura and timeless energy surrounding the event. Do not be confused or misinterpret such things. Everything is eternally flowing: the to and fro of a beating heart of light.

Opportunities for acts of kindness arise in all situations, but most only look with their physical eyes and so many are overlooked. When you live an unconditional life, in unconditional love, then all is opened up before you. Amazing events and occurrences evolve in and around you, so magnificent that some regard these as miracles in themselves.

What can be said or done to activate these wonderful things? Sometimes no words need to be spoken. Perhaps a smile or even a hug to show that you care is all that is required. When someone is on their hands and knees in despair, feeling that perhaps their heart and soul is being ripped into two, what can you do?

Let the love that is you encompass them. Let it be the candle of light in their darkest hour. Shine like a beacon and draw back that veil of illusion and bewildering pain of confusion that entraps, snaring them and grounding them. May your love be their love, when it is most needed? If you believe it to be true, then it will be I promise you. Though sometimes, recognition of this gracious act is not perceived straight away, but it is felt far beyond the senses of the people close by.

Know that in terms of one's development, personal journey, and quest, you will always find me 'within'. There, you will realise that peace and goodwill reigns supreme; nothing can detract from this fact.

You will be the happiest and most content that you can ever be. Such peace cannot be found in the phenomenal world around you, as nothing is permanent there. 'Within', you and I are forever, both eternal and everlasting, a true contentment and understanding of being 'one', no separation or division, for that does not exist there. Such joy can and will radiate for all, and only the timing that takes place on the earth plane, detracts from this.

So, what do the masses or individual wish for at this festive time? Do they wish for peace and goodwill? Many say, "I want peace" therefore take away the ego (I), the desire (want) and you then have (will be left with) peace. So too, by removing the immorality you have immortality and goodwill transcends to God's will.

There is no need to suffer or fear. Have faith and believe and also have faith in yourself and not greed. Share your love, your limitless love, and you will see the effects on the lives around you and also in your own.

See the beauty and the magnificence of the truth and the light within shall then shine upon the golden path to me. I am always waiting and never hiding. My open heart and arms will cradle you in bliss. All you have to do is believe, as I have said so many times before.

I Am I: The In-Dweller of Your Heart

Know me like I know you,
Want me like I want you,
Trust me I like I trust you,
Understand me like I understand you,
Believe me like I believe in you.

Then truly discover me, your secret treasure,
Keeping me close for we are 'one'.
Remember me always in all things said and done,
No separation, no division, just 'become'.

Amen.

LESSON 14

STAR OF WONDER

Welcome once more to one and all, do you see, do you feel, and do you hear my call? I am here, there, and everywhere; even beside you in the next chair. I'm also within as well as out, so do you sense just one heart beat now?

Do not be confused for it's no riddle or joke, nearly time for high spirits but how many choke? Its Christmas time in homes and hearts, but how many Souls still fall apart?

So much stress and why this '*dis*-ease' when one half stands, the other on bended knee. Forgiveness and joy asks many a wish, others look blank as they cross off their list. What shall I give or will I receive, when the truth is revealed in: 'you all get what you need'.

The hungry and the poor, do they cry out in vain, as those who walk by, sometimes glance in distain. Who is the happier as both expressions had met… the rich in the wallet or in heart instead?

You shine as the hustle and bustle picks up pace, there are cards to write and oh, so many calls now to make. Do you radiate and glisten as the 25th draws near, or does the eve and the day bring out dread and a fear?

You each have a choice to glow like the 'Son', each day and by night until victory is won. So now wear a smile or new selfless frown, or the party frocks / new suit, to trade in for night gown?

That's like hiding away so that no one can see, what is the real you and of course the real me? The wardrobe is deep and filled with a choice, garments that disguise like a change in your voice. You can dress up in all, in whatever one likes, but the truth of it all is the world grips like a vice.

Who holds you in place, for it must be yourself, contained in four walls not by goblins or elves. I urge you to walk, to find the chink of light; the way out and then in, it is love at first sight.

Now you can discover new freedom and expression, while open hands lay before…as you realise the new score. So win the eternal goal and move in unison and as one, for all can move on, to then now become.

The pathway was set so many years ago; it was laid out before you, as your Soul and heart know. Many people and new friends then come into your life, some stay single whilst others, take a husband or wife.

You're entwined as one but also fragments of me, as everyone is linked and must return to the tree. Branches and twigs that reach out near and far, your relatives and kin, travel through time, not by car. Throughout Creation and Universe, love reins supreme, open hearts and minds will know what I mean.

Do you trust in me, then search and discover, what lies in the distance, but not undercover. The galaxies and constellations they are too numerous to mention, expand your horizons, isn't that the intention? The Stars and the planets they both mesmerise, but the truth lies inside, not seen with your eyes.

Beautiful and magnificent, no earthly words could describe, glittering prize to behold, beyond simply mind. For it tricks and deceives you into thinking what's best, that false desire's not required, but just love and a rest.

So while looking at sky upon starry nights, what is your wish, go for ground or take flight? Is your head in the clouds as some state you are, or is your heart far above the so called maddening crowd? Just be who you are and what you were born unto be, an expression of love, made of both you and of me.

Do not step back, in shade of past duties or time, rather walk to the glory, of the light so Divine. Every moment or step that you take towards me, I am closer to you, for I have taken but three. This is no ultimatum or difficult test; only wish you that you try, to do your very best.

My grace is abundant and is 'forever' please trust, so having faith in me and yourself is a must. Rise above the times when you cry or breakdown, for I will protect you with my love, and forever my crown. Glory shines down, although your heart may not feel, if you turn your back away, from family or friends who are real.

When you link arms and hands with neighbours as one, the world can then change and it's already begun. This is so hard, for you to see and realise, when violence and hatred seems forever to rise.

Do not succumb, to what media or the politics portray, but do all that you can, to help lead man from decay. Everyday choices and these are your own; so try to lead by example and not by a false throne.

It's in what you think as you strive, along the extra mile, for I am with you always, and am with meek or the mild.

So if you're an adult, a teenager or even a child, what is your dream and what makes you smile? And if you had me, make your one wish come true, what would you ask me and is it for you? More money, a job, new clothes or new life, perhaps change your body but not by a knife?

Do not be weighed down by trouble and strife, or feel that you're unloved because that is not right. For you are everything…and so you are me, not separate or divided for that could not be.

Your essence and your beauty within can't be questioned, no matter what debate or argument is mentioned. You and I both know, of this to be true, simply put we are 'one,' so don't feel down or be blue.

This Christmas time then, please forgive and forget, of the pain or the anguish that karma may have set. Instead be joyful and then reach...out from your heart, for true love is eternal and was there from the start.

And past and present as you decorate your home, live life to the full and beyond speech or the phone. With the Star of Wonder...that you now place on the tree, it represents 'Life' beyond dreams, and you're true 'Reality'.

Happy Christmas to you all, Amen.

LESSON 15

MISSING YOU

Some may feel that after the previous 'uplifting' lesson that they have soon come back to earth with a bump...like a reality check of normal daily living. Why would I do this though?

Well, time and time again during this festive time and as the New Year approaches, I see many hearts will merge in Love and Light with feelings displayed openly, crying in joy. However for numerous people, they wish to symbolically forget the past trusting in the hope of what a change of date will bring as they grieve with their tears of disbelief, fear and trepidation. For those at this time who feel their loved one's (so called) absence, it can be a most difficult period indeed and I understand this.

When two hearts feel as if they have been separated (by body only) and the understanding of such not yet grasped, I sense and feel the pain that is transfixed, piercing outwardly from the 'broken'. The tears that follow those feelings are like sharpened knives pouring out from aching wounds deep within. Their minds numb, emotions raw, eyes are closed while those deafening screams of anguish and disbelief take hold. All of this I feel because we are one. Your pain is my pain and your joy is my joy.

Whether someone's emotions and feelings of loss or of separation are through bodily death or even in the departing of a love one, (be it only for a minute, hour, day, month or year), true love will stand the test of time. This is because the love that I speak of in your hearts is beyond all things. Time cannot erase it and distance cannot break it. You can't manufacture it in some worldly place. You cannot buy it or sell it. You cannot deceive it, persuade it, or cajole it. True love and unconditional love was not and is not born, so it cannot die. It is, was, and always will 'be'.

Those who are grieving at this time of year may wish for hope, asking me to help them or to forgive them for something that they feel they should or should not have done. I will not go into detail of events that could trigger such requests, as this is not required for those who are searching within. They already know.

Across the world in which human beings reside, so many are lost or they just hide. They can also be confused (or are being used) by someone or another. Perhaps ego or guilt also plays its part in those who gaze up at the night sky and look for Divine inspiration.

I Am I: The In-Dweller of Your Heart

Just as a bolt strikes from the sky above, hitting the ground below, people's thoughts travel and can explode into sparks of anger, hate, jealousy, and pride, causing havoc and destruction to those who are directly in the line of fire. Additionally, those sparks that spring outwards can touch way beyond the intended individual or recipient. All of this has consequences, for there is no action without reaction, always cause and effect, both near and far.

When the receiver of such feelings realises what is taking place, what is returned back to the source? All will depend on the soul, whether or not he or she can rise above the pain, the action, the words and the heartache. In such circumstances always think of me. You do not need to ask me for help, to divinely intervene. All you need to do is to think of the love that is within you, that is you and in all beings.

You may ask for forgiveness for another or for even yourself but do not be confused by what I now explain. If I say to you I do not forgive, that will sound bizarre and strange. This is not really so. Forgiveness is already within your heart and so it is not required to be found by some magical act or miracle. I love you and as such forgiveness, when it is in truth, is already there for you.

Hearts bleed in more ways than one and feelings of guilt and blame by another's actions can seem to be too much to bear. The confusion and delusion sets in, so they are then missing the point in what you are truly sensing, feeling, saying, and thinking.

In reality it is 'all' and everything, yet one often thinks you are different to each other with different goals, desires, and wants. This illusion evaporates when the focus is on the heart, as hearts contain the same core essence of Light, Love and me. When hearts connect, it memorizes and becomes all things. It is beautiful and all encompassing. If you could bottle it up it would be called the Divine essence or elixir of life itself.

Consider for a moment those who are separated at this time and now reunite in a wonderful embrace, such as the small child who has been lost, or the child returning from a far and distant place to find their parents waiting for them. Perhaps even the woman or man, a partner and their lover, who have searched for each other to finally see and kiss for the first time. Another example could be those who can't find their beloved pet and suddenly they come back to them. There are too many instances and circumstances to mention.

At this precise moment of connection /reconnection, there is joy beyond comprehension, an out-pouring of emotion and love, radiating like a starburst, a supernova that can be felt and experienced through time and dimension. It is truly beautiful.

For those who read this passage and who do not have this experience do not be disturbed or dismayed. This can be hard to understand or comprehend when the bond of friendship and love seems broken, separated or divided.

Believe, trust and know me in yourself, knowing that all is well. I do not wish any sad thing or for any soul to feel anguish or pain. (I will not go into karma or balance at this point, but the reality of such must be firmly stated).

Upon reaching your goal and your Divine resting place permanently within me, then I say that those that have missed love <u>will</u> also find bliss. This is my promise to you all. Do not fear. Do not worry. Those that understand know that I hold your hand. Those that cannot comprehend do not think you are left behind.

You are not lost and they are not truly lost. All you need do is to remember who and what you are and you will see the truth. By opening up the eyes of your heart, you will see through the mist and doubt of despair to know that I truly do care. I love you and I always will.

Know that this passage was entitled 'Missing You' and that is because after all that I've said, I do. Though how can this be so when I always reiterate we are 'one'? It is because I need you to grow and know who and what you are and can be. Every one of you is unique, beautiful, and there is so much that you can all achieve as individual souls and as the 'one' together.

Whether your lives feel good, bad, or indifferent, if you are in hardship or even basking in success, know that all is for love, only love. Do not despair, do not fear and do not grieve, but remember the tears of joy from the well of your heart.

Those tears that fall from your face, I will bless with my grace. Those feelings of an aching heart that breaks, I will wash away with my own. Be 'still', finding me to instantly feel the togetherness, the oneness of me and of 'us'. No separation, just unity. There you will be purified and glorified forever. You will not miss me for I will not be missing you.

In Love and light be at peace. Amen.

LESSON 16

ACCEPTANCE

Welcome, to one and all. So, whenever the New Year is upon you in the physical and impermanent world, how do you truly feel and what are your current thoughts? Are you glad that you have had the time and space to allow you to think of these things too?

Again, following on from the previous lesson, many of you see the timing of one year passing into the next as a new beginning. You are glad and rather hopeful that you can start afresh, seeing this date more as a pivotal turning point in which to change, with so called New Year resolutions. Whatever reason(s) you are considering, it is important to always remember the saying, 'change the things you can and accept the things you cannot'.

Many factors come into play within this attitude and thought, none less so than faith which we have spoken about before. How you conduct yourselves and how you react and interact with your fellow Souls is important too, as it reflects, as well as resonates, much vibration of Light and Love, but it can also expand disdain, darkness and hate.

Over the past year you can contemplate on much, such as your progress as both a human being and as a being of light. Have you progressed as a person who shines brightly or do you imagine that you could have done more to help others and society? I am not your judge, for you are your own in this respect.

In many areas of your life have you, or do you feel that you have grown in confidence? Do you sense that you are not so much an individual, but are part of the truth, the way, and the life of all things?

I state these sentences now to the readers of this text, as if to someone who over many months has read and digested these words from, through and to a heart. Have others seen a change within you? Do you behave differently? Are your attitudes the same? Perhaps others who are close to you have now formed a different attitude towards you?

Within yourself, can you accept who, what and why you exist, and do you feel any different? Not that I should suppose anything at all of anyone, but consider if you do not? Would someone say that you haven't altered in any way, shape or form? Again, these can be deemed as outside viewpoints and thoughts, but can they be discounted or ignored?

It must be said that no one else should ever try to make you feel guilty, ashamed, or try to pressure you into thinking or feeling that whatever faith or religion you follow is questionable. Only the fact of whether it reflects peace and kindness, as then it qualifies as being truthful.

Indeed, it may be true or be the truth to one and not another, but should your own conduct exude love, then the opinions, reasoning and any outside influence cannot dilute it. It is for this reason that it is your own truth that matters and no one else's.

Also when someone, something, some group of people, government, or country tries to enforce or coerce even one Soul to behave or enact what they are not, then conflict and dissatisfaction takes hold.

This spreads like a cancer, negative energy and stress causing a disease amongst men. But do not fear (never fear), as I continually explain to you. Light and Love is both in and around you and is you too.

This is fact not fiction and above all things. Hence, do not despair when across your world you see, hear or experience what you may call abhorrent or horrific behaviour by a person, group, or nation.

Why or how can I say this to you? If I then reply that, "I do not make mistakes", would you call that arrogance, Soulless or shameless? Would it come across that there is a plan and it comes in some sort of sequence that must be carried out?

In comparison, people have stated before that you could all be actors on my 'stage' of life. Well, what expressions do you see and are looking at upon it at this point of your lives. Who raises or lowers the curtain? (David, you are thinking of the consonants of the word 'curtain'.....you could also think 'creation' instead!)

In the performance itself, are you displaying the truth and true you, or are you like a chameleon; disguising and changing yourself? Is that for your own or for another's so called benefit? Whether you are young or old, there is a part to play, but this is no real game or toy to behold.

It can be said that you have each been given a role, but do not worry or concern yourself if it is a leading part. This comparison with your life, its experiences and expression, need not have the most lines to say to impact or influence others.

Your own appearance can state more than a thousand words. Your heart and your smile can influence and shine far greater than those who appear to be in the limelight and obtain what can sometimes appear as false glory.

You do not need a medal or an Oscar to be recognised by me. In all walks of life, the simple act of taking part is sufficient if you have tried your best and been the best that you have tried to be.

I Am I: The In-Dweller of Your Heart

While you are living your life, suppress the ego. You do not need approval or applause to become fulfilled, needed, or satisfied. All these feelings, in their true sense, are within you. By reflecting upon them, you will realise beyond all doubt your true self. You will witness yourself and view the truth within and out. Then, forever you'll understand who and what I am.

It is then the acceptance of such that will lead you to your goal and fulfilment, your Ascension and destiny. You will become whole and permanent in the greater sense. You will have moved beyond more than the impermanent appearance of 'human' to shine like the Son.

So, returning now to the start of this lesson. The New Year approaches swiftly in most hearts and homes across the Earth plane. Will you rejoice in that you symbolically start or turn over a new leaf? (David, your thoughts again, could this indicate / mean a new 'life' instead?) Can this be a new chapter, a new beginning for each and every one of you? Always, the choice is your own to make.

The slightest positive alteration in your character, personality and conduct can change so much in and around you all. Trepidation and anxiety may remain, but inherent in you all is the ability to radiate and share in the love that is you all.

By linking hands with your family, friends, neighbours, colleagues, and even strangers, or those who need your forgiveness, the New Year can be celebrated with sincere hope and joy for all.

Likewise, when those who come to the end of their earthbound existence and have wished and prayed that they have fulfilled and played their part, may they stand together arm in arm to display unity and peace like a victory bestowed. This will lead to spontaneous applause and congratulations from Soul to Soul, expanding love and light beyond any theatre of dreams.

So, accept the way you live, work and play as you are right now, or become stronger, brighter, more loving, and forgiving. Do what you will and will what you do. Any restrictions are self-imposed; any boundary the individual has set themselves.

You are strong; stronger than you can possibly imagine. No four walls, no false mind, delusion, or confusion can contain your truth, your essence, your Soul. You are not trapped or caged or controlled. Do not think in a material sense for your 'self' is already free to soar as high and as far as your will allows.

If you are ever in doubt or if you ever feel that maybe you're alone, turn 'within'. Be 'still' and find me, feel me, know me, sense me, and believe me for there 'I am'. Acceptance of me and your self will light the way beyond your New Year and forever and a day. Truly we are 'one' and eternal. Amen.

LESSON 17

EXPRESSION

Welcome again to you and all who have drawn close to listen, learn and observe what is written both on this page and also shine's upon one's heart.

Many people from all walks of life upon the 'Earth plane' find it difficult to either express themselves or to 'see' what others portray in their thoughts, words and deeds. As you are all an expression of love, this can seem strange to numerous 'beings' and life force energies that surround and watch over you.

It would appear quite obvious to them that surely, with such beauty and radiance of light within you, that you should naturally radiate love from your heart. However, due to one's lifestyle, beliefs, conduct, and appearance, not only do these ethereal beings find it difficult sometimes to understand you; most people become confused even with each other!

Nearly all of this confusion and misunderstanding actually stems from the inability to say what you feel, think or want to do. This is a denial of self-expression which is often caused by fear of rejection or concern for someone else's wellbeing.

Now, I am not going to say that you should not care for others or worry about another's feelings in your daily lives, far from it. I will explain though, that much of this 'holding back' has so many negative traits that reflect towards your own inner self. These in turn cause you to feel unwell or rundown or worse still cause illness or disease, which is the effect following the cause.

So, what should one do? How should you conduct yourself? How should you interact with others who are close by or even on the other side of the world? Simply, it is the truth and the truth is that simple. In how you think, feel, talk, and act and all the manner of ways to express yourself the truth should prevail.

When you express yourself (this way) with kindness, honesty, compassion, and love, your energy fields 'within' and around your physical, mental, emotional, and ethereal bodies, spiral and dance like seeds blowing on a breeze, and shine brighter than the stars above.

The benefits of letting others know the real you are immense, because not only does it enable you to reveal your true self, those who also witness and sense this will feel the benefit too. Your expression of whom, what and why you exist as a male or female, with different colour skin, of different religious and physical persuasion and so on forms part of your own Soul's picture and is a piece of the Universal jigsaw of 'one' heart.

This is why it is important not to deny yourself and the truth that lies within. It is also important not to be misguided by other forms of 'persuasion', by those who express or even try to impose their will upon you; leading to confusion, delusion and the inherent gift of self-expression being hidden or withdrawn. This would be like a flower being kept in a darkened room, the radiance being confined to eventually wither and fade.

Some of what I convey to you now, like the scene above can be self-inflicted, as if the Soul wishes to deny its own wellbeing and yet still, because of the connection of love, tries to disrupt or hurt others who are linked by any of the four 'bodies' I mentioned earlier.

Such acts are often despised by not only the individual but also others. By all Souls sharing and giving out love, kindness and compassion, many instances of unhappiness can be prevented. It is not appropriate for anyone to judge another, but rather at all times lend a helping hand.

Who knows whether the favour or assistance one gives may be returned even by a stranger one year, ten or fifty years from now, or even on another vibration level of existence, if truth and balance plays its part? Always the choice is yours and yours alone in every aspect of your life.

So, let me ask you, how do you each express yourselves? Do you explain and talk or do you utilise the physical, sending out information and signals through your body language? Both can be meaningful if stated in truth, though it is very easy for those who have drawn close on the various planes of existence to be confused or mystified by what is said or done.

True expression comes from within you, and this guiding light of love which is a 'beacon' strengthens your character and personality. It is through these that the viewer, listener or the participant of a joint activity will come to realise first.

Know that if one relies on words alone to explain or demonstrate their love, it will not fully succeed in breaking down social, physical, emotional, or the mental barriers that almost every Soul has erected or inflicted upon themselves over the millennia. Also, speech itself is too diverse and has too many negative traits. What is the truth and 'nectar' to one person could bring distress and be poisonous to another.

It is in silence you will find the real truth, for it is there that you become the spiritual 'seeker' …knowing that within your experience, comes the real expression of our love as 'one'. By feeling and knowing what this connection is, your faith can become stronger each day and this in turn will enable you to express yourself in your true light.

I Am I: The In-Dweller of Your Heart

Understand that for too long now, human being's 'illumination' has been dimmed by the obscurity of illusion that befalls the impermanent world. Each and every one of you can take a step, no matter how small, away from the darkness and emerge from the shadow of doubt. As one moves forward you will find that it will becomes easier to understand, grow and know more of what and why you are as you are.

Realise that only the individual can make their own commitment to embark upon the journey to eternal bliss and peace. Think of it as a voyage, a continued quest and a mission that you cannot leave into the hands of another. Always it is your own burden and yet it is also your joy, your incomprehensible joy.

For those who have met their 'goal' and who have already 'Ascended', their light shines love unto all. They see, feel and understand you and hear your hearts, Souls and minds as 'one'. They aid you in immense and vastly different ways, expressing themselves in helping, encouraging and supporting you, especially through your assumed 'troubled' times.

Love is the ultimate expression that they give so freely to you all. You are not their mother, father, sister or brother or any person one would care to imagine for they are 'one'. You are 'one' and we are all 'one'. Unconditional is their love, a true love and an expression of which is a sacrifice and the humility that echoes both far and wide; resonating on vibration levels too numerous to say.

Know that those who lie in the gutter will see and know me through the strangers who offer them food and water and comforts. Those that reside in opulence and decadence will come to know me through their own 'expression', if they can discover and acknowledge it in their hearts.

Make no mistake; I do not judge any one of you by any colour, creed or whatever possessions you have accumulated in this world and upon the 'Earth plane'. I do not say that the meek or poor are any better or less worthy of my love than the 'famous' or wealthy.

You are all my heart and only when humanity as a whole expresses love through their hearts can total 'Self-realization' be fulfilled. Please know me like I know you. Your light, your beautiful light, can never be extinguished, for you are the expression and truth of me. Amen.

LESSON 18

CREATIVITY LEADS TO FREEDOM AND EXPRESSION

As you sit and ponder about this new passage or lesson, your whole demeanour slows down as you become 'still'. Your heart rate has dropped, your breathing is more relaxed and as you gaze upon the clouds through the window, time itself seems to drift by much more slowly.

By allowing yourself this moment of peace and contemplation, your physical body benefits greatly from rest and relaxation after the toils of the day. So too, your mind becomes untangled from the very thoughts that help trap an individual into the daily existence of living.

Countless souls often ask me to free their mind so that they can become something more. "Please God, help me to be free" or "Dear God, please free me from this situation" (or event or occurrence). Perhaps, it is to help focus on important issues that have taken hold of them or their family's situation regarding work, home, or monetary aspects of their wellbeing.

Know that this is much easier to achieve than people realise. Like so many queries or quandaries that can captivate or confuse someone, all that is needed is for one to 'release' the senses that you possess so you can 'free' the mind. All the while that the senses 'desire' or 'pursue' in their many forms, lead to the attachment that keeps the mind in control. Therefore, by freeing the mind you can free yourself in your true pursuit of stillness and creativity.

When you are at peace with yourself your light becomes even more brilliant to see and feel by those who are around you both on the 'Earth plane' and in the planes of vibration and ether. An example of someone who lets go of self or ego and who is at peace with what they are and do, can be that they walk into the room and everyone there can sense or feel their presence. It is as if they illuminate and radiate happiness and peace.

Of course, many sages, devotees, Saints, and disciples over many millennia would automatically appear this way. However, I say to you all that the gift of peace that can help you achieve the freedom in your lives is within your grasp.

Over time, the process that I have explained becomes easier, second nature to you if you like. But first you have to wish for it (not a want or desire), for if you truly need it and acknowledge it as such (an important step), then your half-way there. Denying it only fuels the illusion and confusion which feels like your life is pulling you in many directions with cares, worries and stress.

Okay, so now you are regularly 'still' in your life. Now many beautiful things can be set in motion. Some will be hidden and may not appear to come into your view for many of your earth years, while others will hit you like a thunderbolt out of the blue. Do not fear suddenly being hurt in some way, for I do not mean this.

There are many spiritual beings, guides and Angels that watch over you all, assisting and helping in your many karmic actions, as well as just observing cause and effect both in and all around you. Opportunities can be created from your acknowledgement and progress. Doors can more easily be 'opened', whilst people and situations can be guided in your direction to help and assist you on your path and spiritual education.

You are in this 'process' when you can't believe that an occurrence in your life has just fallen right into place and you can't believe your luck! You receive that job offer, you pass that test or exam, you were successful in getting that house which you then turn into your dream home, or perhaps you become a parent for the first time. All these are examples and I am not saying that any of these things happen without your effort too, it's just that as I keep reiterating, if you let go and simply 'be' then dreams come true and miracles happen.

When you are 'still' your inner child becomes free. Your constraints are loosened so that nothing can hold you back. There is no place you cannot be and there is no Soul whose presence can't be felt or seen. There is nothing that cannot truly be achieved if it is held in peace and truth.

As time goes by and your Light becomes brighter, your creativity within expands and develops too. The gifts that you possess (from the power that is both you and I) will be more focused; and your abilities will grow in so many more ways. Remember all spiritual gifts are already within each and every one of you and when you are ready to live in love, share love, and be love, it is always returned tenfold to you.

Of course that is not the reason why you embark upon your new quest to liberation and bliss, but I state this as I always acknowledge everything and all. In terms of action and reaction, I cannot, or rather I will not, preside over to observe and weigh the scales of justice and injustice. These things are already in place for you all to work through and balance out as your lives, karma, and Souls have already decreed.

That said each and every single human being can assist in global Ascension, for fulfilment and bliss. Each person can link hands and hearts with his neighbour, the community, and their country and each nation can realise that they are all one.

Freedom is not something that you need to aspire to, for within, you already are free. The cell or 'prison' of your embodiment is unreal and false. You are the key to open the lock of those imaginary doors that hold your dreams and wishes at bay.

So, as this passage draws to a close, I request that you each be true to yourself. In this truth you will then be true to each other. In the quietness and stillness you will sense me and know me with all your heart, for I hold you in my arms and I will never let any of you go.

Every life and Soul I am. Every atom, particle, chemical, and every aspect of Creation I am. I express myself through your lives. I ask you to fulfil yourselves in truth and Love and Lght, so that from this day forth you can truly express yourself in your life too. Amen.

LESSON 19

FREEDOM AND POWER

Welcome. So, who is free? I ask you this straight away, as it is important for all who read this passage or lesson to think and feel about this. Some may state that it is an obvious question and answer scenario, but you will need to dig deeper, far deeper, into minds and hearts to know the truth.

That said everything is simple because the truth resonates to and from love in all places. The answer hangs over each and every Soul, either as a question or an exclamation mark, which will depend on the acceptance of the light within oneself.

On the surface of the question one could assume that anyone or anything that is not 'trapped' or caged is indeed 'free'. This would indeed be true in the sense of the 'Earth plane' and the way you live at this current time. However, the real issue is not in the freedom where you reside now, but where your Soul's destiny will take it. I will explain this in more detail shortly.

For you all in your current embodiment you're actually living a life of false bondage, an attachment that you have contributed to yourselves. If this were not the case then you would not be reading this at this precise time. Your own karma and right action has, by your own hand and choice, decreed that you carry on learning and educating yourself this way.

As discussed and stated before though, you have an opportunity to attain self-realization and liberation of this age. Therefore, at what point do you acknowledge this fact and start to believe in who, what, and why you are? As basic freedom is 'choice,' then the onus is always on the individual to move forward and become a brighter and lighter being of love.

Throughout the process that you travel upon, help, guidance, and encouragement will be given as your needs arise. Opportunities are created by the meeting of like minds and hearts, which offer windows of clarity and wisdom. This in turn enables the seeker of truth to feel and experience greater knowledge and understanding and this is self-perpetuating. (Just like a small ball of snow that rolls down a steep slope, it gains momentum and grows in size with more snow sticking and coming together).

During your experiences, your growth can continue, stay the same (depending on your inner strength and conviction), or fade and slip away, as if melted by the heat of the Sun. Generally this does not happen very often, but when it does I see that exterior forces and negativity (sometimes not karmic) picking away at the truth and trying to dismantle or bring disharmony to those who may just be 'sitting on the fence' (having that little bit of doubt), and leading to more confusion, both within and out.

By firmly believing and keeping faith in yourself, then you will have more than enough attributes to see the right and wrong in your life of work, rest and play. If you are weak, pray for strength. If you are strong, pray that you may help those who are fragile and need encouragement too.

These prayers, or thoughts of your mind and heart, enable you to realise the choice that is yours in the initial question that I asked you. If you were to contemplate or meditate upon 'freedom' you would came to know a small piece of what it really means and how important it is.

Someone who is held captive is denied physical choices. Perhaps they cannot move about or see daylight or even receive food or water. Any individual who is denied these things may feel that they are weakened, their resolve broken, or perhaps even their life is ebbing away. I say this to you, that in your 'physical' and the awareness of such things as your surroundings, be strong, stronger than you ever thought you could be. You are not alone and never can be! I am with you in all situations and events of your life.

Know too that throughout Earth's history man and beast have been shackled and contained for pleasure, for fur, skin or even for amusement. This reverts to the animal traits or negativity deep within the psyche. In time man will realise these futile actions only bring about death and decay, hate and despair, which have more far reaching implications and effects than is known to you.

You all have 'freedom' and this is inherent from me. You have the freedom to be whom and what you are, in all situations and in all places. The question you must always consider is whether or not your thoughts, words or deeds are in truth or not. Freedom enables you to be kind, generous, loving, and considerate, and a person with values that enable you to be called 'human'.

You have the freedom to express and be creative, enabling you to expand your hand of friendship and hearts of love. These assets cannot be contained by walls or bars. This is the empowerment and the true power that I give to each and every one of you.

On the exterior, someone may see you as a weak person, who may appear to be indecisive, fragile or a 'pushover'. Looks can be deceiving. Your strength is your character of your heart and Soul and this is the truest and strongest muscle that you can exercise to defend negativity. You are more powerful than you could ever imagine. Who can stop your hopes and dreams? Who or what physical structure can contain your love? Even if you are not seen or heard does it mean that you do not exist?

You are all amazing and yet, yes, you do have faults. However, if you learn from past mistakes, your future is fulfilled and your goal of eternal bliss reached. The power within you is so great… if only you accept, realise and then understand it.

We are connected because we are one. In this connection you will find the answers to your questions and find the freedom you crave and seek. Your spark and your very essence can become brighter and clearer every day if you wish it. Your flame of love and light will bloom with petals that glisten and shimmer more beautifully than stars in the darkest of your nights. Your love will become sweeter than nectar and more fragrant than fields of majestic and radiant flowers.

By enquiring about 'real' freedom, you will be encouraging the development of your Soul. It will be enriched through your heart and such gifts will, and can be, shared with all whom you meet and link with on the various planes of 'dimensions and time'.

Many people, who live their lives in truth, touch many hearts in many ways. As stated earlier, often someone may walk into a room and those who are in their presence feel them, for they illuminate and shine energy of love from within their core. Their aura touches even hardened shells.

It is important, though, to realise that they are an example of the freedom of expression. Remember nonetheless, do not become a 'follower' of any 'man' as they still have their own karma to play out. You are the disciple and the seeker of your own truth.

It is 'within' that this teacher lies, awaiting to be discovered. There you will find not only me but yourself, your true 'Self'. There you will experience true freedom and true power that is beyond imagination. Your destiny and your goal await you. Amen.

LESSON 20

INFINITY

Suddenly you imagine a symbol, a sign of the above, perhaps a figure eight leading to an opening, an eternal gate. Contemplation and thoughts and often thinking of your fate, while looking to the heavens, dreams of family, child or mate. So where has it begun? And why does my life struggle when I should be having fun?

There are many questions, both 'within' and 'without', held by the inquirer, seeker, and aspirer of truth. People often look too deeply into what they feel for something or someone who, in fact, may lead them astray, misguide, or even misinterpret what it is they have asked or sought. This is why the full responsibility of their own knowledge comes only from within themselves.

It is, as we have discussed before, the only perpetual and everlasting source of Divinity which is the 'I am I' and 'me'. All else is secondary and will take one only so far on the spiritual path of 'self-realization' and self-knowledge.

Every book and person that you come to know can either push you further away, or nearer to me if in 'truth'. As such, a feeling of resonance 'within' takes place and then, and only then, if it rings true, should you follow it. Always question whether your heart feels it. If you feel awkward, leave it to one side, a 'thanks but no thanks' will suffice.

The expression of 'as above, so below' has many connotations for you all, including the perception of the 'as in Heaven, so shall it be it on Earth'. The balance of the numerous 'planes', dimensions, and vibration levels are everywhere, hence the physical world both receives and sends these.

Energy or life force cannot be crushed, burnt, erased, nor can it fade. It would be like taking something that is forever permanent and trying to make it disappear like a magician's trick. This is an illusion and is why so many are fooled or swayed by disbelief.

Instead, your heart is the truth and my love is the wand that lights the way, weaving and connecting strands of energy to and from you. A magical bond between hearts can't be broken and only the veil of delusion hides your truth from you.

This 'mist' that rolls down from the mountains and hills of your Soul's Karma sweeps in and disguises the true light. You can look, but when you're unfocused, your reality resembles frosted glass with misshapen images and blurred choices and goals. To reach your immortality and permanent infinity of bliss, you need to push aside this untruth and wade through the fog of wrong action to be clean and free again from the bondage of death and rebirth.

If you are experiencing difficult times or problems, such as health issues, family troubles, financial hardship, or are feeling lonely, hungry, or cold, what do you do? Where do you go?

Know that whatever part you play, whatever act or stage you find yourself on, I am the platform, I am the audience, and I am the director of all things. Importantly, know you are not my puppet on a string though you still often look to me (sadly) only in times of strife.

I can be known through and by all of your senses and by so much more. I also experience your joy, and your laughter echoes louder through me than you could know. I mention this to make you aware that I am not impervious to what occurs in each of your lives and hearts. I know you all, better than you know yourselves, and hence comprehend everything that takes place.

You may then ask, "So, why do I sometimes suffer so? How come these events do not happen to them, or him or her? What have I done to deserve this?" Often, no words are even spoken; the smile or tears of joy or pain say it all to me. So, where do the answers lie? And in times of true desperation (comes the cry), "Where is God?"

This query and the outcome (the result), all stem from reaction to action and vice versa. Everything is balance - a positive and negative - and an experience - a cause and effect. I do not point a finger or chastise or hate one above or below another. I do not interfere with what you, yourself, and your karma bring.

Know this; I am not blind to any heart. I am not deaf to any heart. I am not distant to any heart. I am you and you are me so you are never alone. In all situations you know me and can sense me with truth. It is fear that makes you feel further away from me and this is untrue. (Do not be led away by the false fear of death.) Always believe and have faith in yourself, the true faith in me.

Treat all situations the same, as an experience which leads to growth. Self-knowledge and self-realization are the keys to your spiritual pathway and goal. Try to be content and desire only to be with me, forever into infinity. Always, always, always I am there, here and everywhere; knowing you, loving you and aware of every outcome and situation you find yourself in.

Be kind, courteous and helpful to all living things. Nurture nature and each other, perhaps even that stranger. Dispense of your inner enemies of anger, jealousy, hatred, ego, and pride. Go with the flow like the tide, and turn 'within', do not hide. You are all special and each an individual character, yet you are all 'one' for we are all 'totality'.

Be at peace. Do not fret, worry, or fear, just hold me near. Keep me in your thoughts and in your heart for we cannot ever part.

I am below, above and the in between. Hold love in your hearts and you cannot fail to understand what I mean. Be true, not blue, for you are me and I am forever you. Rest in peace and in love and light. Amen.

LESSON 21

THOUGHTS

Realise that there are many people and numerous different beings throughout Creation because life exists upon all aspects of dimension and vibration energies. Some of this 'life' lives alone (in physical terms only, as I am always with and through all things) and they carry on their daily tasks only having to think of themselves.

Within their mind, they act out different scenarios and subsequently their actual thoughts cause 'desire'. From this desire, all kinds of actions are initiated, which in turn activates a resulting function. (Cause and effect) In these circumstances, a human, animal, 'being', or even an insect, gives little or no consideration towards the potential consequences of a single 'thought'.

In such a situation, many triggers initiate these said thoughts. From survival-instinct to self-gratification and everything else that one could think of in-between.

Just consider for a moment two beings, animals, insects, or even parasites which are confronting each other. Perhaps they are in a dense jungle, a desert plain, or deep within an ocean. Say that they attack; hurt or one even kills the other. What thoughts and feelings have taken place?

Some would state, "Survival of the fittest" and could even argue that nature is a law unto itself. Is this nature or nurture? Even at this base level of evolution 'thought' has taken place which has resulted in 'action'.

Scientists, philosophers ,and highly intellectual people of different eras often believe that only humans can 'think', explaining that other brains were far too small, without any real intelligence. Please know thought does not have to originate in the brain as thought is consciousness and can be triggered both in sleep and in an awakened state. As this is so, even minute micro biotic creatures try to stay alive. What is the difference between these and man? Is man nobler? Is man kinder? Is man more vulnerable?

Throughout Creation there are fewer differences between beings and elements of life with man than one would expect. In reality, the main difference is in your ability to feel the thoughts and their consequences 'emotionally'. This is precious and is a gift that is inherent in the Soul. Truly you are all blessed. However, much is wasted in terms of progress due to selfishness and greed for what is impermanent.

Much has to be learnt to move away from this lifestyle and type of existence. Understand that two simple traits that lie so deep within you all can help bring about a real change. These are forgiveness and compassion. Though they have subtle differences, in truth they are the same thing. Deep inside these lie beside the same love that is you and I and makes up all life and Creation.

Do not pigeon-hole these qualities as random acts of kindness. Do not feel that you are above them or cannot show these either. They are as inherent within you as your heart and lungs. They are like your physical legs or ability to move, for they carry you forward through the 'good' and so called 'bad' times that you label as your daily life unfolds.

Earlier we envisaged a scenario of two creatures facing each other, one may live and the other may die. Likewise, human beings on all continents chase or cause conflict on both large and small scales. From a neighbourly dispute to different religions trying to co-exist, there seems to be attitudes and thoughts of 'I must win' or continual attempts to exert control over another. Little debate takes place and actual force is often implemented.

What should be considered is that they are no different to any of you, for we are all 'one'. There is no division and no separation. When this clear and defined notion manifests itself in the heart, it then transcends into thought and right action ensures a positive outcome. It is in this process that forgiveness (and compassion) trickles through as Love.

When a daughter or son is murdered, a father or mother is taken away, a home is destroyed, a livelihood is removed, a loved one is seriously ill, when your pet disappears and in numerous other scenarios that can be contemplated upon, what do you believe in? What thoughts or images flow in your heart? What type of tear is shed?

People will prioritise everything, including other people and their own possessions in their lives. Some may feel their pet is more important than a human being and also vice versa. Strangely, some give even more concern to a materialistic possession than even their own body!

Those that deem themselves as not being physically 'whole' (i.e. missing limbs or a sense like sight) would never accept or do that. It is within all such circumstances that selfishness should turn to selflessness. That a clenched fist becomes an open hand, outstretched to help the fallen.

Each of you, yes each and every Soul, can turn a new leaf right now. Not later, not tomorrow or next week or year. You don't even have to physically go anywhere! You can open your heart to send love and light to all things in all places, if you just believe. Do you?

If you are sincere and your love emanates through your heart then those 'thoughts' of forgiveness and compassion will shine like beacons, sparkling like beautiful stars. As each heart is rekindled in truth, all light that embraces love, then fosters and shares love. These will then join together becoming radiant and magical to be cast out upon my breath as star-dust sprinkled across time, space and all dimensions.

So now, what choice should you make? What option should you take? "Do what you feel and feel what you do" are words I have said upon numerous occasions to all beings since time immemorial. All I ask is that you try to become all that you were meant to be.

May your Soul fly to new heights and beyond your wildest dream(s) and reach for your goal; the eternal peace that is your destiny 'within' me. Remember, everything can be a true reflection of your true self.

LOVE ALL......ALL LOVE.
PEACE FOR ALL......ALL FOR PEACE.
OPEN HEART......HEART OPEN.
REACH DIVINITY......DIVINITY REACHED.

AMEN.

LESSON 22

COMPASSION

"Dear God, please let my heart bleed the love that is both you and I. As many words of wisdom flow in this connection, may they bring understanding, hope and guidance to all those needing your help and love at this time of their lives". DK

Welcome. Today you have heard two sides to a story; an argument, a debate and a brief summary. In over-view, it was a situation that displeased many, shocked some, and yet brought no despair to others. I shall not need to discuss the incident itself, but wish for you to be able to convey the thought processes and subtle differences that transpire within both the hearts and minds of all.

As mentioned on countless occasions, both when you are awake and are asleep, you are all but a reflection of me. In thought, word, and deed and in your body, mind and soul there is no separation or division, and hence the reality is such that you have the ability to focus on every positive aspect of living and being. It is choice and so called 'free will' that dissipates, dilutes, and filters good actions from bad, and the effect from the cause.

When one calls someone else's action perverse or evil, ungodly or cowardly, what needs to be remembered is that whatever the event that has been witnessed, heard, or indeed participated in, can also be the same reflection of what also lies within themselves. Strange to some as this may be, but the difference is the ability, understanding, and indeed the reality of the potential and actual consequences.

Sometimes, those that are not actually aware of all the facts review the scenario with some sort of divine judgement, but all should remember, do not judge or lest ye be judged yourself.

When something disagrees with your belief system or moral viewpoint, do not be quick to condemn, hate or despise another, for who knows what karma has been balanced or erased. This should not be a difficult aspect to grasp, especially for those who embark on their spiritual quest / path for greater knowledge and wisdom of their self and goal.

Please do not believe either that some events occur without meaning, for nothing does or ever will. I know all things and all things know me, as such everything has its rightful place and right outcome for the overall good of Love and Light.

When you are blind, you cannot physically see, yet you can still see the truth within yourself. Because this is so, do not dwell on the negative outcome, but continue to have confidence in yourself and your actions of right over wrong. This means that you have faith in me and as such, you do not and never will, fear anyone or anything.

In all scenarios, your essence cannot be diminished or taken away, for once again I am you and you are me. We are whole, complete, and it is only the false impression, and illusions of the physical world you temporarily reside in, that make some think it is otherwise.

Often in your lives, you will come across situations that your beliefs or thoughts disagree with. When these occur, one simple process that lies within all of your capabilities will always enable you to overcome them. As mentioned before, it is called compassion.

Who is more compassionate, the male or the female? Who feels the bond or ache of love more than another? In all beings this trait, quality, and emotion tugging on heart strings - not from a master puppeteer above, but deep within your core - is love itself.

When ugliness rears its head, darkness and negativity is picking and stabbing your consciousness. How do you react? What should you say or do? It sounds complicated, yet it is not. Everything that is true in life is 'simplicity' and because this is so, the answer, the only answer, is love. Why? Because from love flows compassion and like the reflection, from compassion flows love.

Some actions of other people may appear to be so distasteful that you cannot bear to look or speak to them. How do you know that they are not physically, mentally, or emotionally ill? Just flip the coin and ask about the moral judgement of your own actions today, yesterday, last month or last year. Are there not numerous actions or thoughts that you would yourself have done differently or changed upon reflection?

Do not misunderstand, for as discussed earlier nothing is condoned, but simply realise that until you strive and reach your goal you can only try to be the best human being that you can possibly be.

If you are a mother or father, child, brother, sister, carer, employee, boss, director, an orphan, an immigrant, politician, a King or Queen and so on and so forth, know that whatever are your 'clothes' that you were born into, you should act and wear them with justice and fortitude.

In all endeavours, compassion should prevail, whether that is to your fellow man or the creatures and animals that inhabit the 'Earth plane' too. The colour of your skin and the language you speak bears absolutely no relevance in the heart and heart's centre. True love and true compassion hold no barriers that can ever be erected in any shape or form.

As scenarios develop where a helping hand is required (perhaps someone or something is in distress or ill health) they do not care or think of the helper's looks or colour, voice or religious beliefs or background. Compassion strives not in the clenched fist or raised tone, but in an outstretched hand whether by face or even over the telephone!

One can be compassionate by thoughts, prayer, and just a smile to show you care. By helping others and the society in which you reside, you start to come out of your shell to no longer 'hide'. Perhaps one day you will need another to guide or help you along on your way and journey. Understand that compassion in its many forms will illuminate and shine both to and from you, if you hold truth and love in your heart.

Know too that, within every action, thought, and word is where your heart and true character reside, and both reflect and resonate love. Common phrases like, "so you sow, so shall you reap" and "what goes around comes around" ring true. I am not asking you to be a saint, but request that you take control of your lives so that you can be who you are meant to be.

Do not waste time or energy or money on the impermanent, but seek the truth in all you do. Dismiss desire, want and greed as they will slow you down in your pursuit of righteousness and the glory of yourself. However, your life needs to be enjoyed for you are alive and so all things - as long as they do not hurt you or another physically, mentally, emotionally, or spiritually - should be enjoyed!

You are all one family of Love and Light. Whether you are on different sides of the earth; think, feel and help others. By being compassionate in all that is said and done, there will remain an everlasting memory of the 'One'. Everyone and everything is connected, so no matter how unique or different something or someone appears, you'll see me and therefore yourself.

You are love and love is you,
Know the truth, so truth knows you.
Friends in compassion brings compassionate friends,
Change today and set a trend.

Thick or thin, fat or small,
Head not in clouds, hearts free, not bound.
Glory to me, my glory to you,
We're one forever so live in truth.

I Am I: The In-Dweller of Your Heart

Amen.

LESSON 23

DEEDS NOT WORDS

Since your records began upon the 'Earth plane', people have prayed too many deities, Gods and even the Sun and Moon. Human beings have thought and sent their love, wishes, and desires to something or someone, who they believed would bring Divine inspiration, protection, or guidance to help them in their lives.

All things which emanate from the mind only dissipate upon, and within, the ether. But those sent through and from the heart in truth gather momentum and strength and also reach out and revert from me. Then they attain the required outcome that is governed by Love and Light for progress and understanding.

This clearly defined difference must always be comprehended by the individual and the multitude. It is the conviction that is so, so important in concluding and meeting the one goal that determines your Soul's continued journey through time immemorial.

Whilst so many of you practice your meditations, decrees, and prayers each and every day, which is so important for the wellbeing of yourself and all elements of life, it is but part of what makes you whole in your persona and character. Because of what we have just understood together, you can now leap forward and grasp the wider picture of who, what, and the why of your daily lives in thought, word and deed.

It has been well documented about simple analogies such as 'actions speak louder than words' and it is this that needs to be viewed slightly differently today. This is because so many people will feel that they have done enough by requesting support in numerous different ways, i.e. spiritually, materially, physically…not perhaps for themselves, but also for those around them too.

What needs to take place is the actual personal involvement, for truly the 'deed' takes precedent over the 'word'. You yourself have learnt the expression, 'Hands that help are holier than lips that pray', this is because whilst the prayer is universally felt as a vibration of love, the physical body that contains both your heart and mine carries out, or indeed enacts the actual process itself. Reflect upon this for a moment to establish deep within you this truth that beholds you all.

Throughout life opportunities will come and go, some of these you will have utilised and others you will miss. In essence, openings which offer help to others will be created not only by me but also through the actions and decisions you make. When they materialize and are taken up, then light vibrations dance like diamonds and crystals, reflecting sunlight sparkling all around you and the event or action which has taken place.

This is true in all places of existence and cannot be diluted or defused by negative energy, darkness or hate. As love knows no bounds, it will forever be seen and felt by all hearts that are not blinded or encased by illusion.

Because Love and Light is so beautiful and so simple in its entirety, the amazing thing is that no matter what deed or act is carried out in peace and truth, the same effect *always* takes place. So, whether one helps an insect that is struggling, fallen over on its back or whether you travel across the street, town, country or the other side of the globe to help feed the hungry, it is always felt both within and out.

People have often prioritised insects, animals, people, and the world into their own pigeon holes, each having their fate or lives held by individuals or religious belief systems. Only when the penny finally drops, that all are one, with no diversity and separateness, then humankind can begin to ascend as 'one', together in unity.

Currently, decade after decade of your earth time passes by, with only the few attaining Ascension and their eternity in me. If, throughout your earthly incarnations, many more had began to open minds and hearts, acting godlier in all they say and do, then billions would be within the permanent state of love and not the impermanent world of physical vibration.

Please do not panic or fret yourself though into an early grave. All that you need to change is there within and around you. Look, and more importantly understand, the openings and opportunities that are created for you in your daily lives. Do not strain and think you can't see them, but focus on what you think, say and do, for like the jigsaw pieces that come together, you will then see the true picture in all its glory.

Do not think badly of people when they do you harm or are angry with you. If you have tried your best in all that you do, then becoming what you actually really are is inevitable. Some may think that this world is too far gone to realise the dream, but it is not and never will be out of your grasp. That said, if your 'helping hand' was seen and understood to be right in front of you, would you reach and take it?

I am with, within, and besides you, so you are never alone. Together we are one and by opening your heart you will feel and know me to return where you really belong. Do not worry when things apparently go 'wrong' in your lives. Do not fall down and say you can't get back up again, as that very hurdle could be the last one you need to overcome.

If your life becomes unbearable, please think of me, trust me, and have faith in me. If you have confidence in yourself, **all** these things are easier to bear and I will carry you. Please put effort into being the best person and being you can be. Follow the truth, say the truth, and enact the truth as we have discussed all along.

You are all only bound by yourselves. You can only be deceived by your own 'false' self. Advice and guidance from many sources will come into your lives. Some are right for you and others only for those that have balanced karma and are ready. Take only on board that which feels right for you as an individual. If it rings true to you, then you will resonate 'within'. Then you can act upon and grow with it, but more importantly, help others with it too.

Sow the seeds of Love and let the deeds of action and truth multiply far beyond the walls of your home. The barriers that have been falsely erected will fall, others will hear your call to feel and know Love and Light is all. You are all eternal and I see, know and love you. Amen.

LESSON 24

'TRUST AND FAITH'

Welcome again to 'stillness' and some contemplation time, enabling you to reflect and clear those thoughts that can block clarity, which in turn brings you peace. The working day is done now, so be still, feel and rejoice in the calmness of your true self, for you and I are 'one'.

My love washes over all, but many cannot feel or sense and more importantly just 'be', to actually appreciate and grow within it. All will do so, but not until they realise who, what, and why they are a spark of Divinity.

So tonight in your Earth time, you can now pause to let light and truth rain in. It will cleanse any doubts, fears, or misapprehensions that you entertain or those that have sneaked up upon you this day. Do not concern yourself with minor ills or worries, for these are trivial when all is said and done.

I often hear some say that when these occur they are being 'tested' by 'Spirit', perhaps to see one's reaction or to establish one's inherent code of conduct and whether this prevails or not. Friends past, present, and future have stated that you, the individual, or the masses should 'rise above it' and of course it makes perfect sense.

Do not let yourself be led astray by negativity, by another's hand, or by those who do not hold truth or love in their heart. Remember, this can be achieved in a diplomatic way and not in blank refusal or with a curse from the tongue.

Inside of all of you is the truth. If you live in truth then recognising all ill-fated or incorrect paths or actions will become easier every day. Being positive attracts the same, where spiritual education and guidance is concerned. The expression opposites attract is only true of the physical, impermanent world in which your embodiment resides at this time.

So now I ask you, do you trust yourself? Do you trust in how you feel and think? Do you know your intuition and those 'gut' feelings? If you do, then place yourself not only in trust of your 'self' but also in me, then you have acknowledged the unbreakable bond that connects us all.

With trust there is no fear. Having no fear brings you peace. In peace you find bliss. In bliss your permanent true self shines like a supernova with magical stardust spiralling and spinning in all directions. Mere words do not, and cannot, do justice to such beauty.

Opportunities throughout your lives will come and go so please grasp those that ring true and resonate within you. When tasks are embarked upon with, by and in truth, then nothing is impossible to be achieved. Only the limits that an individual proposes to themselves can prevent the ultimate goal of Ascension being attained.

By trusting in all that you truly are, you can reach far beyond the stars. Limits and boundaries are falsely erected by such insecurities of an illusionary mind. Push these aside with the love that is you. Trust me to give and help you with what you need and require, not in what you want and desire.

As I have described on many occasions, you do not need to travel far from your home or disappear deep into a forest to discover me. To find me is not difficult for I am already within and outside of you, as I am all things.

I am the stars at night shining light through the darkness. I am every leaf and rock. I am earth, fire, water and air. I am the wind that brushes against your face. I am the peace and tranquillity you crave. All these I am and in truth, you are too. No separation or division, only oneness in all.

People's thoughts of doubt and despair however can still linger both on the 'Earth plane' and on numerous vibration levels of energy. "How can I believe? What proof can you provide for me? Why do you let so many suffer in pain or anguish?" Understand that many hearts ache or break which I see and feel, for I know them all.

In truth, all of your ills and concerns could be washed away in an instant. Yet you all (on a Soul level), know that this is not the way that you truly learn and grow, for karmic balance cannot be alleviated and achieved this way by any mortal man.

It is Faith that can guide and carry you throughout 'life' and it's seemingly impossible burdens of work and family and your general wellbeing within society. Many religions from scores of nations use faith cart-blanche, and it has become almost like a byword or phrase to indoctrinate people's hearts and minds.

I am not stating that people throw away <u>any</u> aspect of a religion or cultural inheritance that they have grown up in. Nor should any life be decreed as more sacred than another's. I only ask: who or what do you believe in? Also, who or what do you think you <u>should</u> believe in? Does your current thought process and belief system enable you to be who you are, deep within?

Now, I do not wish to antagonise or offend any being or life, but only the truth and its reflection can make someone or some place feel this way. Rather this; believe me and believe in yourself. True faith of (and in) Love and Light is so magnificent, powerful, beautiful and amazing it knows no bounds.

Throughout your history sayings such as 'faith can move mountains' have been heard by the many, but how deep has this truth been buried over the centuries and eons of time?

My message from this day forth is to dig deep into your spiritual core to grasp and behold this true golden nugget. Keep its truth and power close to you every minute of every day. It will never ever let you down, for as you search, pray, and through your actions, words, and deeds of love, I will polish, smoothing the rough edges of your Soul's experiences.

Have faith in me. Never doubt me, for I do not place doubt in you. My strength will be your strength. My love is your love and my light is your light. You will shine eternally within me and your essence will forever be permanent. Show all you meet the truth in you and be a guiding hand to those who doubt or fear and who do not have faith even in themselves.

For all those who are still unsure, I request that a leap of faith does not require you to risk your health or loved-ones or anything at all in your wellbeing. It is but a gap, a space, that seems to exist between you and I and it is unreal. My love for you is an eternal bridge that cannot ever crumble. Seek me and take just one small step, for I promise you I will carry you forever into eternal bliss. Amen.

LESSON 25

TRUST IN YOU AND ME

I am here and know your thoughts even before you have perceived them yourself. You wonder about subject matter for tonight's lesson and whether your connection and stillness are prepared and ready. Do not worry, fret or be concerned, just trust in you and me.

Throughout your daily lives, from the moment you awake until your head lies down to sleep again, numerous choices and tasks that you will do become conspicuously concerned with anxiety and worry. The majority of which can be removed and extinguished in an instant if you let one thing enter your heart's centre: trust.

If you have trust in your own actions, or in someone else's, it will alleviate many disturbances from your mind. These afflictions, if left unchecked, can lead to all sorts of negative traits such as stress, ill health, disease and decay of the body. This in turn will affect you on more levels such as the emotional and spiritual 'bodies' that you possess. (The reason being is that you become trapped within a circle of questions and doubt, constantly wondering of this, that, or the other).

What I mean is that, instead of letting go and becoming free from the decision or action involved or taken, you will always be thinking whether you have done the right thing. Worries such as, "What will happen if…" or "If only I had…" and so on. When you can't let go, or are afraid of a consequence, then trust fails to exist and the effect will follow cause.

So, who, what, and where would you feel comfortable in letting go of concerns and worries? Is it in your own home? Is it in the presence of family and friends? Please know it's wise to trust, for like the mirror, its reflection will become true and wash over you.

The question remains about the level of trust you can give both of and from yourself. Material elements, such as your possessions, should not even enter the equation for they are impermanent and of no real value where spiritual education is concerned.

You may strive to 'own' any manner of items such as a car, house, furniture, televisions; but in reality, even though you feel that they are yours, 'citing' how hard you have worked to possess them, they are but a transitory and fleeting pleasure. I am not saying that one cannot be successful or live in a warm, comfortable home with so-called mod-cons, but I request that you contemplate the meaning of them within your life at this current time.

I Am I: The In-Dweller of Your Heart

I am also <u>not</u> stating that you give up any comfort or family security, but wish for you to re-think, or more importantly re-prioritize, what is beside or within you so that your outlook (the vision that you sense and feel both in and out) could change for the better. Therefore, the question of trust falls both upon the individual and the many. Do you trust what you feel and think, or does your mistrust cast a constant shadow within your life.

As your life and what you do with it involves many other people, the fear is that someone will be let down. By allowing this feeling (that you do not trust another), then you become like a caged bird, forever facing bars in all directions which then prevent you from taking flight, a journey beyond the 'self' to me.

By its own premise you will feel worse by missing opportunities to shine and grow (from illusionary fear). Even when the cage door is open and freedom beckons you to stand upon the threshold to immortality, you wait. Yes, you wait and wait and wait as if actually requiring someone, something, or even an event to say or state, "Come on then, you're free. Come this way, come to me".

In all lessons and structure of any religion I will not do this. Know that I am not contradicting myself. My helping hand is a heartbeat away, but first you must recognise it yourself and take the steps to freedom and bliss, yourself.

As a child takes their first 'baby' step, then the action of trust is its equivalent in spiritual education terms. By developing your trust in yourself, know that the trust and confidence in me too, will soar.

Eventually the bird is free to fly, majestically soaring high to reach places that can only be dreamt about. I will be your other wing to enable you to do these things. Together we can achieve all that you want in the name of Truth and Love and Light.

However, be aware that your 'Earth plane' existence and embodiment will often be tested in numerous ways. First and foremost in the trust you provide and give to others. Sometimes your trust may be misplaced and sometimes your trust will be abused or misgiven.

I state, do not despair when such things occur to trouble your heart and mind, but rather let them wash over you. Refrain from taking the bait and becoming entangled in the false communications and actions of others.

In these circumstances and occasions it is better to 'rise above' the disruption and any inconvenience someone or something has caused you. This will enable you to focus and re-concentrate on the truth, and you will be able to hold your head up high, displaying true human values in all their glory. Think of these times as 'minor' inconveniences and do not make the proverbial 'mountain out of a mole hill'.

Remember, that balance and karmic balance always prevails. In time, you will see your own pathway clearly ahead of you. In your life, you will know what feels right for you and your intuition will play a big part of this. Often you will sense if something that you are saying or doing (participating in or by thought or word or deed) is right or wrong. Trust in this too, for the feeling is a link to the truth that resonates with you. People, over a period of time, become very astute this way and it becomes second nature to them.

As I have said and discussed before, you all have the attributes and abilities to succeed in your life 'within' you. You only need to start believing it and believing yourself to then believe in me.

The word 'trust' is small. The definition can be as complicated or as simple as one can wish to make it. You can dismiss the idea altogether or you can take the first 'baby' step to joy, peace and bliss. Know that just as that child first stands, a hand is helping lest they fall upon their knees. As I am within and with you at **all** times, I am there, here and everywhere to help you in your endeavours and tasks upon your enlightened path.

Take a step through, to, and with me, and your life will change forever. Trusting in me, and to trust in yourself, are certainties, for just as the Sun rises to a new dawn each day, I will illuminate your path with every breath that you take. Amen.

LESSON 26

FROM 'CHILDHOOD' TO 'ADULTHOOD'

Welcome to another 'lesson'. Although we have briefly discussed and gone through parts of your 'stages of life' before, today will not just be about the physical aspect of one's progress, but also the emotional and spiritual development of your being.

Where should one start? Some may say, "At the beginning of course", but I would reply, "So when was the beginning?" This is because you were all never really born (other than into your past and / or current physical embodiment), so this does not actually apply at all. We are 'one' and so fundamentally separation or division has never entered into the equation.

However, because of your Soul's development and history of action or karma, there must always be a start, a beginning, or a birth for it to progress and understand who and what it is. More importantly, of what there is to achieve too. This is of course the 'goal', the self-realization and liberation of your Soul.

So, to become permanent from the impermanent, the Soul undertakes freely and with all that they are, the quest for fulfilment and bliss. In relation to the physical, you may not comprehend this until your further progress and development… in passing through the stages of life.

These stages are easily signposted as birth, childhood, adolescence, adulthood and retirement. If you can imagine a container with golden nuggets stacked upon each other, then the comparison is clear. The container is yourself and the layers inside are the evolution of your being, which in turn is your character and appearance as well as the emotional, mental and spiritual aspects of 'within'.

At birth you cry, which is the defining moment that you have comprehended your rebirth into the impermanent physical world. Understanding this means that it is quite clear why you would cry! On the 'Earth plane' the doctor, nurse, or midwife may seem be the instigator of the cry, 'to clear the airways', but this is just cause and effect taking place.

So, you are born again and who knows whether within your karma that it is but for only a minute, a day or a year. Perhaps even three score and ten? Time is irrelevant. Birth could be for the purposes of your own Soul or for the benefit in aiding those who are around you, as a group or Soul 'families' also play their part. In a previous lifetime you could have even been a next of kin to your current siblings.

I Am I: The In-Dweller of Your Heart

The important thing to know is that in your birth mother, you hold a debt that can never be repaid. All earthly debts can be repaid, earned usually (or sometimes otherwise). To your mother who has carried you, always there will be a need for gratitude. That said, all your actions towards your parents should be respectful. It should form part of your individual 'human values'.

During your childhood and adolescence you are learning and growing on many levels and through your experiences, actions, and thoughts, which can be positive or negative. Education plays a major part in personal responsibility and your character. Some may find that they are quick learners and others slow. If you're best efforts are always given, no one else should not feel that you have ever under-achieved or unfulfilled your potential.

The important issue here is to do with regrets. How many would or will look back and feel that they missed out on opportunities throughout their life? (Which could for example, be with their education). Not fulfilling dreams and aspirations can haunt a person as they grow older stating, 'I wish I'd done that, tried this or that'.

This said, many so called 'famous' people, or as you would say 'celebrities', have little or no academic background. Do not be confused here, as karmic balancing may be the reasons behind either success or failure. The secret is to accept the highs and lows, the triumphs and the defeats, the praise and criticism in equal measure. Do not fret or fear or be excited in the so-called sad or happy times. Do not waste energy on 'feelings' that are transparent and translucent.

Be able to hold your head high; not with ego or pride, but with the knowledge that self-esteem and good character is worth your weight in 'spiritual gold'. 'Within' you can be as rich as a king; while the 'exterior' that people see (with closed hearts), could be one of a pauper.

Remember, appearances, especially physical, can be deceptive and by listening to what resonates within you, truth will be found. It will guide you constantly as your days pass by, seemingly quicker, as your body ages.

Reaching 'adulthood' physically, of course, does not mean maturity. Many reaching great age still find that they still making petty remarks and actions, perhaps regretting what was said or not said (or done) at a later date. However, emotionally and mentally, ideally as one ages you should become more flexible, tolerant and adaptable to others around you, no matter what their misgivings.

Through your 'later' years, if your efforts and work have come to fruition, you may be able to help people in many ways. You do not need to own a mansion to think that you can now finally help others. Some that are poor or even in ill health often serve in society as well as for those who are deemed 'better off' than themselves. Choices are always yours to make, with your integrity, honesty, and wellbeing, but you can decide if any or all are at risk.

Does what you read and digest make you feel any different? Do you feel justified or even inadequate in any way? Please always remember the love and kindness that each of you have and are. In doing so, the answer to any query or quandary that perturbs you will come to the forefront of your mind, enabling you to think and act in truth.

Of course, the other main point to consider in your life stages is your spiritual education and development. People often assume that this is a separate issue, but of course it is not. As your days pass through these stages of work, rest and play, opportunities always present themselves. These occur from your own actions and the influence of others, as well as aid and help via spiritual guides, Angels and 'Light workers' from and through me.

In search of truth and enlightenment, and to reach immortality and bliss, you not only need to grasp them with the proverbial 'both hands' but more importantly with an open heart. You do not require, or need to seek a reward from any earthly source, for you are blessed with my grace.

Your life stages may be governed by colour or race, by fame or fortune, your spoken tongue or by the shape or size of your physical appearance. Whatever your condition, and wherever you are (and also however you find yourself), remember the unique opportunity that I have empowered within you. You can make your ultimate dream come true and no 'man', institution, government or earthly power can withhold you from me. I love you. We will be together forever. Amen.

LESSON 27

SIGNPOSTS

Good day (God day) once again. This time that has been set aside is a bridge, a connection, an eternal love.

As you walk upon the path of this 'lifetime', the road can seem rough and very demanding, physically and mentally, as well as spiritually. This may seem as if there is separation, but there isn't. All have equal parity on the quest and journey.

There will be times that walking this path will also be smooth, as if you are gliding upon air. These experiences and events of such occasions bring joy and happiness to both the individual and, of course, to the many guides and Souls that watch over events of the phenomenal world in which you are currently active.

When these good times are happening, many just accept them as normal occurrences and yet much is taking place for this to unfold. Many vibration energies and karmic balancing produce those moments within one's life. How much is taken for granted by those whose heart is not truly open?

There needs to be awareness and also appreciation to your own innate Divinity that helps you experience such things. When this takes place, the Love and Light within expands and radiates far beyond oneself, touching, expressing warmth, beauty and overwhelming peace. By opening to the true 'self', then we are truly embarking upon the road to immortality. What does one need to look for to know the truth and the road of bliss and serenity?

By opening the eyes of the heart, the way is lit before you and the path is marked out for every junction and turn of your lives, as a signpost. Can these be read with physical eyes alone? No. It would be like asking the half blind to view an object on a horizon, with dense fog all around them.

It is this eternal mist of illusion that should be cleared as soon as possible. Then, the steps will be easier to take, and each stage of your road will be lit with a beacon, your guiding light of truth. Pure love that shows you the way never leaves you and it does not distract or lead you astray. It beckons forth, lighting the entire road ahead to reveal any danger or distraction, until you realise the eternal 'home' of pure joy, peace and comfort.

Signposts can come in many forms, not just as your imagination thinks or believes. Everywhere and in every situation comes the split-second or judgement of the Self. Those pause for thought moments. Should I or shouldn't I? This way or that, left or right, up or down, in or out? Indeed there will always be simplicity and simple answers to confusing or complex scenario's that you find yourselves in.

Much has been said and discussed in literature before, with such debates about going with the flow and the sixth sense, but try to go beyond this. Let your heart decide, deep within, whether something feels right or wrong. Do not worry about consequences, for if you have offered your actions to and for 'God', the results are my burden and mine alone. However, remember sincerity in all that you do, think and say.

You need to become 'still' to feel me and to truly know me. It is then that my peace will wash over you, lifting you closer to your goal. I am the sword of protection, I am the warmth, nourishment, sustenance, and everything you could wish for or need.

When you are unable to be 'still', then feel me in the wind, sunshine upon your face, and raindrops falling upon your cheek. Know me in the mountains, valleys, and upon the seas. Wonder of me in the stars, far off galaxies, and sense me in the smell of a rosebud. Also, as birds fly and animals roam the beauty of the land, gaze far and wide but search 'within' to see all these things and so very much more. Everything you know and have experienced is but a fragment, a minute atom of all that I am (and of what you are).

Be near to me. I will lift your heart when you are sad and I will smile and laugh with you when delight passes through your soul's experiences. Do not worry and fear, for I am always near. In fact, I am nearer than near, for then comes your understanding of the 'I am' you and you are me – indeed the living tree of life. So, I am the words upon your lips, the sights that you see, the pain, joy and every experience and moment that you were, are, and will be.

Sometimes you may sense angelic forms close by you. They watch and see all of my Creation, never judging, yet all pervading. They see 'without' and they see 'within'. They enhance the beauty bestowed upon all things and they are there to help you when required to do so.

Light Hierarchy of Angels and Archangels, Ascended Masters and Souls have earned their wing. I am the balance that lifts and carries all too where truth reigns. I am their other wing to help them fly. Know that as you are me, you are all things, and there is nothing that you cannot achieve in your true heart.

All you have to do is to decide what to do with the time you have been given upon your 'journey' in this lifetime. Look for me on the outside and 'within' for you will find me on display, not hidden away. You can rise into my eternal heart and taste the bliss of true peace. I am the silence within the noise; and if you pause, you will hear this 'quietness' of our one true beating heart. It is an eternal heart that forever feels, knows, carries and loves you with all that I am, and of who and what you are. Look for me and see the many signposts above, beside, near and within you.

Remember what you are, not born or created, but everything that ever was and shall be. In your weakness I will make you strong and in your strength you will conquer fear. By conquering fear and worry, you break free from the confusion and illusion to find immortality. It is for all, so realise and become it. Be at peace. In Love and Light, forever 'I am'. Amen.

LESSON 28

THE 'LESSON'

Welcome. So, you all seek to learn and this itself could be called the lesson. Know that each and every 'being' in their various ways and paths of life, and in whatever plane and dimension they reside, cannot but grow and learn.

Some may say or have said that there is only so much you can learn in any one way, through books, pictures, or from the lips of another. Is this true or untrue? All sources of learning from within are infinite and yes, you have learnt and also do learn through what you call passages of time.

In and during 'time', you will all grow and understand the true meaning of evolvement and enlightenment. It will be different for each and every one of you as all souls are unique, individuals, yet you are also all 'one'. Your light already existed and you digest and breathe light even though the levels of vibration may vary.

A soul's brightness depends on the truth and the love within one's heart and one's heart's flame. It is this that sustains, maintains and moves that individual to new and lighter planes of consciousness, dimension and learning.

So, even the dullest and faintest light, which could be called a fragment of me, can grow and learn the 'lesson'. That Soul can remain as a lower vibration, even in obscurity with its artificial loss of freedom, power, and free will. That said, even if that pathway or choice is undertaken, through a monumental effort to grow and learn forthwith it can still be done. Only the lower 'self' prevents this.

Likewise, if the Soul strives to achieve fulfilment beyond its wildest dreams, it can grow and learn to new levels of vibration and consciousness only by its free will and desire to do so. This again is a lesson in itself.

From the time a child picks up a book or a Soul glances into its heart to take a look, new evidence of its learning is taking place and takes shape. All grow at different rates so, although one may say to another, 'I know more than you'... is that really true?

The answer is no, for the exterior knowledge gained is but an illusion. Only knowledge that manifests itself deep within the heart is true wisdom and growth. So, when the book is read, perhaps in one's chair or bed, or even if a lecture is given to those who listen with their ears, do they really grasp what is flowing from the source or does the information flow to one side, leading to pretence, blindness, and confusion?

Only when these things touch an individual's heart can they be said to be of any usefulness. This may sound strange to some but will be understood by those who not only use their bodily senses for normal living, but who also expand, opening their hearts and minds to love what is within the light and which is in all things. Does this ring true or does it make you feel blue?

Do not feel downhearted and do not fall down on your knees to the ground. You may go to the altar of a church, kneel and look into the Heavens and pray, but unless you pray from deep within your heart, you are only sending energy and a vibration containing no true rhythm.

If your heart is true then the signature of your Soul with its rhythmic state can be heard and felt across all dimensions, time, and space. No barriers or fences, nothing to fear, override or overcome because all is near. Yes, both near and afar and deep within too, for the light is you and it remains true.

Of this church, do you picture four walls, a tower or a spire? Or do you envisage yourself within a body, mind and soul? This altar that is spoken of is not a marble slab but of your own heart, cradling your soul's living, violet flame. Would you come to your altar unprepared? Would you kneel with the fear of being burnt and back away, or would you step into the flame of truth and peace everlasting?

Know that your soul's flame is unique and so beautiful. Its construction is the key and the truth is inside for both individual and global destiny. The flame does not burn but is made of light and peace. It contains all wisdom of yourself and Creation

I do not give you any less or more than each other. It is only the false perception that your neighbour or family member is better than another. In what way is this judged? In what way does that reveal or show you the real truth? Does it push and shove or gently nudge you, the individual, to come to this altar of truth, peace and of love?

You each have the choice and free will. I do not say do not come together or congregate, but ask you to question yourself, your truth, your desire, and your reason for congregation. Togetherness is important but do not be misled or misconstrue whom, what, and where you are, for when you pray from the heart it does not actually matter.

You can never be alone and you are never alone even though you think that you sometimes are. As you are part of Creation and part of me you can never ever be.

You are all 'one', in various forms and guises and you're all part of truth and love forever. It is this recognition and this understanding that the lesson leads you on to greater knowledge, wisdom and the comprehension of the 'All' as well as your destiny.

The lessons on these pages, with these words and letters, give meaning and understanding that, as the pen writes to leave a trace, eternally open your heart to love, so that no tears ever fall from your face. Remember, you are true love and light so be 'still' and now take flight. Amen.

LESSON 29

1000 ('I's)

Who is the 'I'? Don't you see?
Where am I? I am thee.
I am you and you are me,
Not born and yet, both from the tree.

So many eyes are searching far and wide, looking, feeling, wanting, and hiding in shadow, when all is light around them. Over mountains and land, sea and air, I carry you in my heart, for we never part. We are one, always and forever. How can there be division and separation when you are whole? It is this recognition and understanding that is so important and I will keep reiterating it for you all.

All you have to do is be true and still, to feel and know me. When you are calm and your mind detached from illusion, you can hear your own call that resonates to and from me. Look into self, the heart of truth, and let it reflect your own brilliance and self-perpetuating love; divine you are, Divine you'll stay.

Do not let the senses of the body dull your goal and one true aim of eternal bliss, that of my embrace and kiss of peace and tranquillity, which is beyond apprehension. Search with the 'I' which is beyond hesitation. Search with the 'I' of truth and find me in every leaf, rock, and in all things. I am the core, the 'In-Dweller' in you, (as you are in me) and by my grace, I will help you to truly 'see'.

Human beings in vast numbers have eyes that are open yet are still blind, for an invisible eyelid clouds the vision of the heart within them, binding them to illusions and delusion. Through and from love this can change, and it will change, for I have decreed it to be so.

As the river of time flows by, know that it is only I that can ease you to the safety of the shore and into my loving arms of peace. Look for me in all you do and offer all you do to me in truth. Believe all that you do in thought, word, and deed to be an offering to me both sacred and pure and as stated before, all consequences of your actions will then be mine.

Right action, through right body, gives right karma. All are one and the one are all. As they are entwined, your body causes action and every action is karmic, so be true in all you do.

Let the flower of your heart bloom and the petals be fragrant with your love and Divine presence. May this aroma sail on the wind and fall on 'life' both far and wide, touching many souls across many tides. No distance or time can stop or prevent love and light from emanating and illuminating all that I am.

Whether a single or even 1000 'I's' gather in my name, it makes no difference to the strength or brilliance of the bliss that is felt upon realization of the 'goal'. Know that I am aware that so many beings think that the goal is to reach a heaven. It is not, for in essence 'Heaven' is only one stage of progress further than your material or phenomenal world in which you currently reside.

Once you cross over and all your right 'actions' that you have accumulated in your previous embodiment have passed, then you choose to return back to the 'Earth Plane' (Unless you have previously cleared 51% of your karmic imbalance as many well now comprehend). This is why your true goal of immortality within bliss (your so called Nirvana) 'within' me should be striven-for in all ways.

So now then, how do you gain your immortality? Lose immorality! Be a worthy human being and not an animal or beast of anger, jealousy, ego, attachment, and envy. You have earned that right of your body, to enable you to reach your immortality.

All the other 'beings', animals, and living things in all of Creation have not reached this stage. Be blessed with my grace and truly accept this opportunity that you have wanted deep within. Do not waste your days, for it is too late when your body and senses become weak with old age. How do you think both you and I should feel when the question of your own life and mortality comes to haunt you?

I am not berating any individual but just to tell you of the truth: the earlier you begin to awaken in this embodiment, then the easier it is to become and reach self-realization. When your ability to understand and the senses (used in truth) are sharp, they can become much more easily focused on the goal in question.

Be near and dear to me. When you gaze out of the window, see, feel, and know me. When you contemplate Creation, understand and behold me. Then, when stillness befalls you, realise all this is within and truly is you, for I am you and you are the 'I'. Love will purify all when you yourself call. Go now in Peace and Love, to and from 'I'. Amen.

LESSON 30

ENLIGHTENMENT

Short and fat or tall and lean,
Come to me to truly 'see'.
Black, white, yellow or red,
Do the living walk or are hearts all dead?

New horizons glow,
As the Sun shines down,
But how serious are you all,
When so many frown like clowns?

As this text reverts to rhyme and reason,
All human Souls flow across nation to nation.
All individuals, or are they really?
While global communications link 'satellites and telly's.

As someone views to take a look,
Others read lines from numerous books.
Each one seeks the answer to their life,
No matter if you're a son, daughter, husband, or a wife.

Information and guidance sought in a digital age,
But few still seek the wisdom of a Sage.
Throughout all time, Ascended masters came and went,
All born Divine, but some were burnt at the stake.

Who can you trust, to find the answers you seek?
Do they lie with a guru or the mellow and meek?
Open your heart to be still, and really see the glue,
Know that I am I 'within', and am the 'me' that's in you.

So no need to feel it's such a mysterious link,
Always gentle and loving and more than you can think.
I will not shout or remonstrate and scream,
For love lights the way and I'll show you what I mean.

I Am I: The In-Dweller of Your Heart

Unveiling this in truth is a test and a task,
"The first steps unto bliss?" you might as well but ask.
Now illumination and Divinity they go hand in hand,
In unity we fall and united we will stand.

So now it's all for one and one for truth and all,
The loudspeaker and a hailer now bellow out the call.
These words upon a page are a voice of sense and reason,
Be it day or in the night, of each and every season.

In spring, summer, autumn, or the cold,
I am the way and the door, the true spiritual gold.
Nuggets to inspire and to teach, oh yes, to guide,
Revealing what you know and the answers are inside.

So open up this book, to read or peek and look,
From my heart I hope that now, you are truly hooked.
The Light, oh yes, is growing with steady pace,
The brightness glowing too, as your heart falls into place.

Illumination so beautiful and it is, oh, so bright,
Lasts forever while awake or in deep sleep in the night.
As dreams and images flash, both in and on your mind,
They reveal in every way that we are one of kind.

So, whether you now run, or walk or even crawl,
Upon stage of love and life, it's no matter tall or small.
As character and your essence can play a little or big part,
By day and also night, your choice is from your heart.

What you then but see is a reflection of yourself,
Do you admire or condemn and stay stuck upon the shelf?
By growing and in learning, the reincarnation act,
Performances of this life, as you're now right back on track.

The light then shines on truth and not upon the lies,
Take a bow and the applause and now my glittering prize.
This is not a trick or any man-made gift,
But enlightenment bestowed, to reward your own true grit.

I Am I: The In-Dweller of Your Heart

Time and time again, you may have fallen down,
And tears may have you dropped as you rightly wear my gown.
As you enter now my kingdom you'll be escorted into peace,
A winged chariot to then carry you, draped in Golden Fleece.

Then sitting besides me now, in my heart and not a throne,
Remove a ring of thorns, replace with a true crown.
I have empowered each, in every one of you all,
Ascended Masters like my Son who awoken to my call.

You too are my love and my light that has so grown,
So fly back unto me, back to your permanent home.
Do not fritter or belittle, what is rightfully your due,
Just hold your head up high in whatever you do to.

The light that is you all, it cannot tell a lie,
So grow in to the truth and try then not to cry.
Sometimes 'bad' things happen, to those only that do 'good',
Sometimes it's the opposite, but you doubted that it should.

Do not fret about, of what is yours or what is mine,
For all that is now needed, is the Universal sign.
"But what is it?" Some now ask and pray,
"Is it magic; in these notes, the Divine to save the day?"

No wand or any crystal or mineral or fool's gold,
Can ever shine the 'light' and of the glory that is told.
Whether you really believe or you think this is a 'fake',
I still love you even though, your re-birth is at stake

Don't dwell upon the negative but carry on as you please,
And walk the line ahead, for 'you' I will not tease.
No emotional blackmail but free-will I ever send,
From darkness came a voice and words of light upon a pen.

I wish for you all always, for great things to then achieve,
But I'm sad when one gives in, to desire or to sleaze.
The want and the need are but tricks upon your mind,
Times like these be 'still' and you will then be fine.

I Am I: The In-Dweller of Your Heart

Overcoming doubt, and the false despair,
Shows each other that you feel, and truly that you care.
And if you do succumb and fall flat upon your back,
Know that I am there, to keep you right on track.

So many lines of vibration are very near and clear,
For I am within all things, so far and also near.
Go forward in real motion; but will destiny then wait?
Hearts of Love and Light, to cast out all doubt and hate.

Books and many pictures, from now to bygone age,
Each tells a true story in their lines upon each page.
Some just give a whisper or even a small peek,
But truth is the beholder, of the heart that you all seek.

I think that you'll agree that in these darkened times,
A fragment of some hope can come in glint of an eye (I).
A sparkle and a beacon, perpetual joy is not a sin,
Your eternal goal connects, but not only from 'within'.

I ask you then and now, with the all and that I am,
To try to now 'return', a wish home in this lifespan.
Choices forever will, and always will be yours,
Step onto life's bus ride, the only magical tours.

Destination is unknown for so many of you its true,
But never doubt in what you are, and of what you all can do.
You are truly everything and so everything is you,
So fulfil your one true goal, knowing dreams they can come true.

It's time now for a rest, for the hand upon this pen,
The words circulated on the ether, beloved I have sent.
Be at peace and May the light; shine to and upon you,
Together enlightened hearts, stuck together Love just like glue.

Amen

LESSON 31

UNITED

Welcome. Be still and find the joy and peace within yourself. Put aside the rush and frantic pace of the day to write with truth, the truth that is one of you and me.

Many of you, from the moment your physical awakens, are moving at a breathless and breakneck speed. It is as if your being is on 'auto pilot' which becomes almost robotic. Things to do, people to see, places to go, the list never ends.

These scenarios are on top of seemingly endless cares of work, rest, and play and, more importantly, those of your family, friends and distant kin.

Let's pause for thought, moreover, have your thoughts on pause. Just 'be' and in letting go, this can be vital so that you can realise that you are part of Creation and not separate from it.

Much of your activities are about the worth of others and many things in the material and impermanent world. However, what or whom considers *your* self-worth?

Again, this is very important because your own Soul needs to be recognised and not pushed to one side. What real value do you sense or give upon the real you? Do you think you are worth less than the next person? The answer is, of course, no. Then why do so many of you act as if you do and are?

Your worth in my eyes and your own heart is not in what home that you reside or what vehicle you drive. It is also not measured in the clothes you wear. Neither does your race, colour, or creed have any influence whatsoever.

Your Soul and true self is revealed from, through and to love, and the connection to me is unbroken by time or space and dimension. It can be said that we are 'united' in love.

Your Soul is revealed through your heart's centre and, depending on your life and karmic balance, will shine in beautiful plumes of colour and radiating crystallized pink.

However, should your imbalance be so severe through generations of self-abuse or neglect, for whom and what you truly are, then a shadow, sometimes grey or deep black, will surround your heart, like sticky molasses which takes much time and effort on your part to remove.

I Am I: The In-Dweller of Your Heart

You must understand and grow in the knowledge and wisdom that you are worthy of my love and the goodness and truth that is all around and within you. If this was not the case, then why do you exist? What would be your true being and purpose?

You need to be self-accepted and also love yourself. Often people will say, or you may have heard, that unless you do these things it is hard, if not impossible, to accept or love another. Do not fear what others may think or say of you. Just act and be who you are and not what people want the reflection to be. Always, you need to reveal the true you.

These attributes will aide your creative energy and spiritual gifts that lay hidden deep within your psyche. Often they are dormant until such time that even you may say it's too late now to express myself.

Being positive is crucial in negating such thoughts or wishes or traits. Do not succumb to trickery of the mind's desire to tempt, or pull you away in directions that are unimportant and misleading.

Shatter the illusion and confusion when this occurs by acknowledging such an event or situation. Do this by being your own witness to state: "I have learnt from this and I can move on from this now".

Many times in your life you will come across events and occurrences to test, unnerve, unseat, and knock you from your comfort zone. Expect them, for you cannot gain wisdom without the experience and this knowledge.

So, where does this leave you? Do you tune into your true self or your 'ego' self that wishes to make you believe just in the here and now? Rise above the attachment and temporary fulfilment in many areas of your daily existence.

Look at, with, to, and from yourself. What do you see? What do you sense and feel at this time about your true needs, your hopes and dreams? What are you prepared to do to achieve your goal, your journey and your Ascension?

I cannot answer these questions for you. That is for you and you alone. Do not be influenced by any other Soul upon the earth plane. You can take advice, read any book, visit any sage or scholar, but ultimately your truth will never be theirs and vice versa. Your truth lies within your own heart.

You can reveal it to whoever you wish, but you can never portray it as someone else's truth. No one should be pressured into believing anything said or done by another. Always, the truth is in the heart of the beholder.

Individually, you are all holders of the truth within your own hearts. It is a sacrifice and needs your endeavour to know, feel and grow with it. Embracing the love within is the only way, for it will lead you to me.

I Am I: The In-Dweller of Your Heart

By being 'still' and meditating on the truth in your own heart, you embark upon the journey. This stillness is like a boat upon the ocean of love and it will carry you on to your destination and rest for all eternity. Do not worry about oars or sails to steer you or to speed you along, as my grace will do that for you.

Have faith in yourself for, as I have stated, you will then have faith in me. It is all you will need. This vessel, your physical body, will come across many turbulent seas and storms, but with your strength and conviction these can be *easily* overcome. Knowing the truth will bring you to calmer, clearer, and shallower waters.

This will enable you to travel over great distances more quickly. What I mean by this is that the distance you travel is really the wisdom you gain through the experience of self and life.

Again, do not worry or stress when times get tough. Treat the so-called good and bad with indifference. You will receive what you need when you need it, no more and no less. I do not and never will abandon you.

I am the shoreline that guides your path back to me. I am by your side and upon every wave of emotion that emanates from your heart. Sometimes you will feel as if your boat is going to upturn or perhaps flounder upon some hidden rock. Ignore these feelings from the mind and follow your heart instead.

Then within, you will come to recognise me as your true self with no hidden agenda or meaning. Love is simple and truth is simple. Simply 'be'. I will cast aside the turbulence of any troubled thought that tries to pull you down; you only have to understand this in your heart to know it is true.

One day or night when you're Soul has acknowledged it; you will all ascend upon the radiating coil of light emanating from your heart to mine. Your vessel will no longer be required or needed, and hopefully it will have served its purpose and served you well if you have looked after it.

You will then come ashore, for you will have remembered me above all things. Your hand will be in mine with our hearts entwined and united for all eternity. For you will have recognised that you and I, your true self, are 'one'. I love you all, always. Amen

LESSON 32

HEAVEN

Welcome to the stillness and my love that is shared with, to, and from thy heart's centre. As the peace encircles thee, a love radiates within, spiralling and rotating, an energy beyond all comprehension to many a Soul or mind.

There are many questions that people have etched within themselves and this beckons the yearning and aching for answers, or perhaps an 'answer', to define all things. Sometimes, people are afraid to even contemplate such reasoning, an innate fear holding them in a vice-like grip, preventing them to escape the seemingly never- ending cycle of birth and death.

It is sad that I hear so many on the earth plane asking me, "What is Heaven?" or "Will I go to Heaven?" All these queries are asked not just by the elderly who are in their twilight years but often by those who are embarking on their new journey of discovery too.

This 'journey' could be of the outer senses, which encapsulate travel and the like, but also those who suddenly find themselves just wondering. This can come about after a tragic event or in so called 'losses' that they feel over the passing of a relative or a much loved pet. Maybe this enforced 'inner' journey will lead them to greater understanding or belief, a stronger faith, or even just the reverse if they blame me for not intervening or helping in the situation that developed.

Many, many things can be felt and experienced if the heart was just more open. However, lots of excuses can be bandied about like there's "No time or no point" or worst of all, "It's a waste of time!" As I feel all things, even an individual's thoughts and feelings touch me. I feel your joy and I feel your pain. 'I' am all I am and as such, like a mirror, I reflect all that you are and can become. What vision, scene or image is reflected to you and your Soul? Can you feel me? Can you sense me?

Thoughts can turn dark or they can shine the light that remains hidden within by so many of you. Each passing day, billions of Souls work, eat, and sleep 24/7. Where is the time set aside for the truth? What plans are made to reach your true goal, your resting place of your Soul?

I am amazed at so few searching, yet numbers are growing and will continue to grow steadily. All it takes is trust and faith in me. Get to know me in all that is said and done in truth then, as in the title of this note and lesson, you will experience Heaven.

So, will people be thinking of pearly white gates, Garden of Eden, the akashic records or even of a man with a white beard sitting on a golden throne surveying all and sundry? If I explain that Heaven can be what ever you want it to be, many will gasp or shout, 'What rubbish!' Perhaps a set idea or memory or even a picture in their mind has been embedded for far too long.

Religious teachings of all faiths profess to explain or insist that you do something or achieve a level of goodness-knows-what to be blessed and welcomed by my grace. Well, many sages (of all the ages), have never been in the position that all of humankind find themselves in now. This lifetime is unique, an opportunity, a gateway to bypass so much grief and heartache, to lie in my embrace for eternity. I have decreed it and offer it to you all.

No one can say he or she is better or more religious or more loving than another. As you are all me and I am you, then there cannot be any division or separation for we are whole. As this is so, who can deny it upon themselves to turn away and become blinded by doctrine teachings?

You are all free to choose who and what you can become. Nothing can change this. I request that you search 'within' and find the Heaven that you seek. There is the paradise, the unconditional love that exists, emanating from all things. Live in me to find me and all heartache, problems, and stresses will disappear from your troubled mind or heart.

Just for a moment, imagine your favourite place. It could be anywhere, at any time, anything. Perhaps you find yourself beside a clear blue sea, walking on white sand or sitting by a crackling log fire in your favourite chair. Maybe it is in your lover's embrace or it could even be solitude, high upon a mountain, surveying the wide vista on a clear day.

All these elements are thoughts and feelings within you already, though some will say you would have had to physically experience them to recall them. This does not concern me. It is the inner peace and wellbeing that is conveyed at the precise time and moment your senses touched your heart, that is the only important thing. So, this is a Heaven too; which indeed is the joy, calmness, peace, and beauty, as well as the understanding of it all through the love that is forever me.

Realise that when the body dies and you leave it behind, your Soul embarks on its journey and truth is revealed. Within that precise moment, I can also sense and instantly know the peace and the reflection of all that the Soul has experienced and achieved. That is your karma ('action') and your heart, as well as everything that you have learned with memories. Yes indeed, all things.

You will know this too, so have you achieved all that you require or wanted to? Did you meet your goal? I am not your judge or puppet master, but am your eternal friend and confidant. I am you and you are me as I will continually define. If you haven't met your desires and your wishes, do you remain within the peace of Heaven? What would then become of one's Soul?

Simply, you have chosen to return to the physical embodiment, no more, no less. Once all good deeds are balanced out and karmic energy of the previous lives experiences are erased, then rebirth will occur. Some who read this will raise eyebrows and say, "What, going from Heaven back to Hell then?" Know that words can mean nothing to some and everything to another.

I request that you live in the 'present'. As I have explained on numerous occasions, it is the gift to you all that I have 'pre-sent'. Grasp it, be who you were destined to be. Reach out from within yourself and both share and experience the Love and Light, the eternal me and you. You are all things and all things are you. Live it and believe it for it is true. For now, love and remember to be 'still'. Amen.

LESSON 33

MIRACLES

Oh my Son, brother, heart, and love we are 'one' and nothing and no one can divide, separate or cut us into two.

Everyone is whole; they are not just part of the 'one' for they are already complete. This must be understood by everyone for all too correctly progress and justify 'in', into, and beyond the 'truth'.

So many Souls are still taking baby steps when, in reality, all of the human race could be leaping and bounding to their goal. I am not criticizing, but educating those who are unsure of themselves, their 'self' and 'higher self'.

Often, people see small nuggets of information in various ways, some common and but some known to all. For example, in lectures, books, films and the like, and yet so many have not tapped into their golden heart of Love and Light. It is here and only here that the unwavering reality will sink deep within their very core. Then, they will understand the one true miracle of undying peace, beauty, bliss, and Nirvana that is me and you.

This miracle (and indeed the coming to this realization) surpasses all Creation. This is because the tiny plumes of flames within your physical heart (which are too small to be seen with sight alone, for they need to be seen with the eyes of heart, mind, and Soul in unison) are directly me, the source of all things. As this is so, everything else is impermanent and forever dying and being 'reborn'.

The permanent Atma, Soul, and light within can never fade and die and is as beautiful and majestic as it always was. It is what is around, hiding and covering it with layers of the sticky black molasses of Karma and time that betrays and falsifies. Unless the individual 'body' blows these away through right conduct, right action, truth, and love, then ones true being remains blinded, consciously and subconsciously, until small and more frequent changes are made.

Someone can change this very second or it may take years for them to comprehend the why, what, where, and who they actually are. What I am explaining is that you do not have to wait one lifetime more. You do not need to be 'reborn' ever again into physical embodiment. This is the choice for all, each and every one. However, who and how many will take up this challenge that they have actually set for themselves?

Each person can achieve their heart's desire and make their ultimate dream come true, but will you? By keeping me near and dear and by wanting to know, feel, need and love me, then I will remain a reflection of those wishes. I am not distant from you. Will you distance yourself away from me any longer? I am not just behind, in front or beside you, but I am within you for I am you. Recognise me and you will recognise 'you'

Think for a moment about your family, friends and pets. Perhaps they are the centre of your life, this bond and the love that you feel for them. Do not be afraid or unsure of what I am about to tell you, for all these involvements and relationships are very important because they help you grow and flourish as a human being. Compassion, togetherness, trust and so many more qualities can be expressed between these links.

However, this is all attachment. You may think you love your dog for your dog, but you do not. You love your pet for yourself. You believe you love your wife, husband, son, daughter, father, and mother for them; but you do not... you love them selfishly for yourself. This only causes anguish and heartache. So how can you love them and yet, when they depart, let them go without grieving? (As their 'essence' is not actually dead!).

This will be understood when your knowledge, experiences and understanding of what and who you really are makes sense to you. When you know me 'within' yourself, then all the answers to queries such as these become simple and are simply put to you. True love and light and understanding is not complex, it is simplicity itself. You will comprehend this and follow this through your heart and life ahead.

The miracle of me is you, and the love that is 'I' is you too. This is therefore the true miracle. Love is everywhere. It is who you are, and who and what you will always be. Remember this eternally, for even in your darkest hour I am there, for I love thee.

When you are 'still', know me as the air that fills your lungs, as the breath of life. When the sunshine falls upon your face, know that I am here, there and am forever in every place. When you hear a bird song like a gentle lullaby, know that I am within you always, never to say good bye.

When you smell the fragrance from colourful blooms and petals, know that I am the true scent that perfumes your heart. When you see spectacular natural phenomena, know that your gaze has seen but a fragment of my power. When you touch and wipe a tear from your eye, know that your Soul bleeds the truth that is your 'self', you and 'I'.

Let the resonance and vibration energies of peace and truth continue to shine and grow. Overcome negative feelings and false emotions; try to stop them in their flow. Continue to be 'still' and you will be taking within the sweetest pill. This is no Pavlov's dog, no false or hidden pretence, but it will sustain, help and guide you. Always, always follow your heart and in doing so you will know mine. Remember:

Love and Light goes to all - All go to the Love and Light.

Amen.

LESSON 34

FEELINGS

Welcome once again. Do not fret about tiredness and responsibility of your day, for I will strengthen and empower you to overcome any negative thoughts that emerge from your body, mind or Soul. By being still, you will feel at one with yourself and me, and thereby become focused on the work at hand.

Your conscious and unconscious mind sometimes hold you in a spell, making you think or feel that you are not moving forward or progressing in some way. Many people often find this in their lives, feeling that they are not achieving or setting the world alight in the search or goal.

Please listen all of you. I say that you should never be too hard upon yourself. While it is important to shine your light and love from your hearts, you often still forget to actually show or express the truth.

What I mean by this is that in expressing how you actually feel, you are revealing the true, inner you. It is essential to talk calmly and with honesty, so that whether the words or moment come from anger and hate, or with compassion and mercy, the true you and truth prevails.

People may ask, "But how can it be right to display your anger?" In reply, I would state that it is only a reflection of self and hence the real question should be; "How can I rectify what I have said or done, that caused you to be so angry with me?"

Do not feel or think this as strange, for if you have accepted that you are all one, then no division or separation occurs and you will realise that feelings of so-called good, or bad, contain all things.

Your mind may switch to the blame scenario, that it was someone else's fault. In all the daily acts of your life you will come across such events and have interaction with other people who irritate, annoy or who are rude or discourteous.

Please do not look at the failings of others, but rather overlook them. Rise above these negative situations, with their apparent ease in which they can intimidate you and others around you. Do not judge them, but offer the kindness of your heart, which in turn will reflect and magnify their own light, piercing the shadow or cloud lingering over them.

I also see in many hearts, the suppressing of true feelings or deep subdued emotions, due to the fear of self-denial or fear of offending others. It is a fine balance that needs contemplation upon, and in clarity of thought there lays the truth, to enable you to proceed with dignity and as a person and Soul with true human values.

People can often act strangely and out of character. Their behaviour becomes weird or bizarre, but why is this so? There are many reasons that explain this, but most will come from stress, which is 'dis-ease'. Pressure one may feel can surface in various forms, and people may recall numerous occurrences when they just snapped.

Two important issues are raised here, one being how the person is conducting themselves towards you or others, and secondly, your reaction; the effect following the cause.

It is true that the feelings and emotions displayed by another could have a large impact on the resulting consequences, but all events and their outcome will be influenced, for better or worse, depending on the wisdom of those around them at that time.

Anyone can make a situation that appears hateful or spiteful turn around; with a smile, a softly spoken word or by offering a helping hand of love and peace. This is a choice that the individual alone can only make.

So, how do you feel at this moment within your life? Do you feel bitter, annoyed, let down, confused and perplexed or with a heart that blooms and radiates love: feeling contented, blessed, happy and fulfilled?

What does it take for you to feel the latter? What do you need to alter and change within yourself? It can be easy to change your partner, job or home, but these are all external. It is the interior that needs to be redecorated with hope and faith.

Please believe in yourself, always. I promise you that if you have confidence in yourself, you will never look back. Do not ever doubt the love and light that is within you all. It is there, it is forever, and it is beyond your beck and call.

My grace flows over all life, from the tiniest creature or flower to all beings and all of Creation. Is it favoured? Is it rationed? Those that think or believe this, please look deep into your heart, for you will truly know me there and you will find your own truth and self too.

How you feel towards me shows up in your 'make-up', ranging from your personality and demeanour to your very spark of your life. How you feel about yourself is also a reflection of how you feel about me.

Therefore, whether you receive praise or condemnation, whether you are rich or poor, whether you're clothed or naked, know that they are all feelings and elements of the exterior.

Imagine a circle for a moment, what do you currently think of? Is there anything within the circle? Are you outside of the circle? Do you believe that you cannot enter it? If I was the circle are you outside of me?

I Am I: The In-Dweller of Your Heart

Am I unattainable?

If you believe that you are on the outside, does it seem like you are looking in upon many situations of your life? I urge you to take control of your lives and believe with all that you are; you can win and achieve the true goal, the goal of Ascension!

Do not misinterpret anything I have said, for I want you to be happy. True happiness is not (ever) to be found in the impermanent or physical world, as you will always continue to be tempted and tricked by the mind to desire.

You can truly 'feel' when you turn within, there is no other way. When two people fall in love, they do not worry about what others think or say. They only know of that special feeling that seems to make their whole life flow. They are within themselves and within the moment. It captivates, sustains and fills them. True love makes any separation feel unbearable.

Even though we are all one, millions of Souls project this feeling to me and yet millions more distance themselves. If my heart was physical, it would surely break. However, my heart encompasses all life and all things and as such, knows all outcomes, situations, thoughts, and feelings of every Soul.

As I am light and love, I am all power and all Creation. Hence you can realise that I am your breath and heartbeat, so when you feel the way you do, I do too. Therefore when you talk, walk, work or rest and play, express your true feelings so that others can share theirs. Always when your thoughts, words, and deeds are given in truth, all consequences will be taken upon by me.

Do not fear or worry, for I am within, without, above, below, in front, and behind you. As I have stated many times, you are never alone. I love you with all that I am.

In your past, present, and future, your feelings leave traces of whom and what you are and can become. The tears of truth will fall from eyes and hearts until all Souls know that we are not apart, but are simply parts of the same living flame that burns eternal as we are all forever 'one'. Amen.

LESSON 35

PERSEVERANCE

Human beings since time immemorial have embarked upon many trials and tribulations. Some of these are personal, others for their families, town, city, nation, or for the world.

Within man, woman, girl or boy there will always come a point where an event or task that they themselves (or even others) have set. Choices will be made, ambitions realised or failed and a victory or defeat then ensues.

One could say that in an attempt of any kind, even if it results in a failure, is not a mistake. It is true that learning will be inevitable in such cases and it is down to the individual whether they strive forward or not in their endeavour. This leads us to analyse and even accept human failings as well as those times when congratulations are due.

So, when a person feels drawn to any numerous different paths in life, be it artistic, business and financial dealings, exploring the depths of the seas or jungles, and even the vast array of jobs and service to society, everyone will think upon what they have actually achieved over time.

Please do not misunderstand that if someone does not create a masterpiece, become a director of a huge company, find lost civilisations or even become the best shopkeeper in a village that they have failed, either.

No one should judge another, whether they are king of the jungle or if they fall head first into the gutter of life. What I hope you will comprehend is that it is oneself that creates your dreams and aspirations and it is yourself that either denies or glorifies you in the outcome.

Many expressions come to mind such as 'reach for the stars', 'make your dreams come true', 'pick yourself up and dust yourself down', 'when the going gets tough the tough get going' and so on.

People can have many a goal in life that they want to achieve. Others simply find victory in actually just staying alive or keeping their 'heads above water'. None the less, each and every one on planet Earth needs to pause and reflect on what it is they need or what and why they find it is so important.

Some want to build this or that, others wish to find a cure for a disease, some wish to climb mountains or trek the globe whilst others may simply want to be the best parent they can possible be. Whatever the task or endeavour, there will be a testing point which will materialise. Whether your focus is taken away and resolve severely tested, old obstacles may be changed or even multiplied, and during this entire experience one may question yourself, your sanity, and reasoning, but most importantly your faith and hope.

I do not and would not chastise anyone, but often when this reality or situation hits home, it is the person's confidence and faith in their own self (and in me) that shines like a brilliant star, or dimly like a candle that burns and fades.

People could conclude that in times of fear and trouble that I do not hear or come to aid thee. As I am you and you are me, we are 'one', and I know, see, hear, and am all. As this is truth I know of both pain and joy, and of victory and defeat in equal measure.

I do not place one above the other or am concerned whether opinions of right or wrong should prevail. How could I? How can I? If that was the case it would imply that I love or care about one Soul over another or in Light over darkness. All are whole and there is no division.

Physical 'experience' only pretends that this is not true. Remember that physical embodiment, although so very important to live and function on the 'Earth plane', is not permanent and hence brings about the illusion we have often spoken about before.

So, where does this now lead? Well, it can or will lead you to where you want to be in your heart or you could dismiss it until a greater or more urgent interpretation sets within. If you decide that you want to achieve your destiny, you have made your first step upon the bridge of light and the connection, the 'Pathway' to bliss and permanent life in me.

Then, throughout your life, every second, minute, hour, day, month, and year, by being true to yourself and to love 'within' and around you, your life will be more at ease both with yourself and all those you meet. You will see me in all things and in all places. Joy will flourish while truth and peace will grow and flow like a fountain sprinkling love and goodwill wherever you are.

You will be content and this will ease your mind from the desire for impermanent things. Your understanding will develop and finally comprehend that it is not yourself who is the 'doer' of your fame, fortune, wealth and health. Also, in serving society, you'll know that you're actually not just serving others, but as each and every one of you are me, then you are all serving God and hence yourselves!

Do not fret when troublesome times come, but rise above things that, upon reflection, will seem trivial and not demanding. Aim to live and walk in truth and, more importantly, in and through love, which encompasses everything. Stride towards your goal and persevere, especially if others seek to cast you into negativity or darkness, for you will realise that victory is but a heartbeat away.

Don't sway in your conviction for you know what is required. Should doubt ever rear its head, be 'still' and turn within to see your true self once more. Let the Love and Light shine through every fibre of your being, physically, mentally, emotionally, and spiritually. Think of these as one, for you are truly whole.

Remember also that every step you take, every place you walk and in everything you do I watch over you. Some may say "Huh, that's like 'big brother' or Orson Wells 1984, so could this really be 'Hell'?" Life and your destiny is what you make it. Know that you can achieve your permanent goal but only through your own efforts and perseverance in this lifetime.

Ultimately, know that I will never leave you. I cannot let one Soul pass by. How long it takes is down to your heart, Soul and the life you lead. You are Divinity and you are light so be and flow like an illumined seed that blows on the breath of life. Forever we are 'one' and we are 'one' forever. Amen.

LESSON 36

'APPRECIATION'

Welcome once again. A few minutes ago your thoughts expressed a wish for me to draw close to you and reveal words of wisdom. You also requested that love be shared to, through, and from you so that others may feel the same love and happiness that resonates from 'within'.

Well, your consciousness became aware of me as soon as you became 'still', didn't it? At that precise moment what filled your senses, primarily your hearing? It was wondrous 'birdsong', wasn't it? The notes were so soothing and calming to the ear that all other exterior 'noise' was forgotten. Now, silence befalls you covering you like a blanket made from the finest silk, helping you to focus and concentrate on the task at hand.

Okay, now that this is the case, you re-glance at the top of this page of text to ponder upon the 'title' of this lesson, 'Appreciation'. You could be forgiven in thinking that this is to do with gratitude of (or for) services rendered or in the outcome of a certain event in your life. Well, I would like you to go beyond this in terms of your thoughts and these generalisations.

First and foremost, you are Soul, Spirit or the essence of light and love. Therefore, upon your acceptance of this and your understanding that your physical presence is but a shell, an impermanent 'home', it should be easily grasped. However, in this conclusion it is vital that the 'body's' importance is not called into question.

As your mind, body and Soul are 'parts' of the whole, they should still not be considered as separate or a division of such. If this were the case it is very easy for someone to conclude or devise that surely one was more important than the other. While you are on the 'Earth plane' this can never be the case.

So, all three can help you to discover and feel the beauty and peace that exists 'within' and also in the 'without' (or exterior world) in which you live. To be able to register the sensation of such, it is imperative to be free of pain, stress and disease. This is so important for you to comprehend this because it is very easy to be confused and mislead by karma and balance within your lives.

Your body is a temple, a haven and an amazing reality of existence but do you really appreciate it? I state this because those who (for whatever reason) have impaired judgement through mental, emotional or physical conditions may be (currently) unable to influence factors which have a say on their bodily condition.

The body should be kept fed, clothed, and clean with a balance made between exercise, play and work. You yourself can be in control of these things where your free will is allowed to exist. In these 'situations' you can only question and therefore answer to yourself if you have over-eaten, become lazy, inactive or have become ill from overwork. Everything is about balance and each of you has the necessary tools to weigh up the pros and cons of your thoughts, words and deeds.

An example of this would be over-indulgence, just having that 'extra' which you often regret afterwards in feeling lethargic and bloated. Your stomach should always be able to cope with physical and emotional conditions if you accept the following consumption; ½ of food, ¼ of water and ¼ empty, a principle that many sages and devotees subscribe and adhere too.

When the health of body is sustained, then your sense and awareness is so very much heightened. This also stems from contentment and a happiness of whom and what you are. This will enable you to be creative or a creative expression of love and light that manifests itself into the impermanent world in which you currently reside.

Understand that there are many elements of 'light hierarchy' that help Souls to achieve this, such as Angels and princes of light. Through your love, thoughts, and prayers they can help manifest the conditions and opportunities for self-expression in your home, work, and the environment in which you live.

When you sense beauty (in whatever form), be it nature, a person's smile or in the hope and love that you experience through mind, body or Soul, how does it make you feel? Do you stop to consider it? Do you ever question it? Do you appreciate it?

One of the key elements to this lesson is that through the 'body' you can therefore 'experience'. This then provides wisdom, for it is then practiced and confirmed 'knowledge'. This is a gift, a present and an opportunity, or it can be deemed a trial, tribulation, or 'hell'. Remember the exterior is a reflection of the interior. Do you see snow white or a wicked witch?

A subtle play on words, but nonetheless the meaning is conveyed. As you go through your daily life do you see the negative or the positive? Do you sense all of one or part of them both? Do you just see other people's failings or are they a mirror image of your own, hidden or twisted into contorted views?

Perhaps you can see the glory in all things or maybe you can't. I do not judge any one of you. Deep within it is written upon your Soul's Love and Light that you are perfection. By removing the rose tinted glasses that cover the eyes of your heart, Soul, and mind, it will reveal and erase the false sense of reality, so you can then witness the truth.

Beauty is not in the eye of the beholder but it is the 'I' (true self) of the beholder. It is only when you can let go of the past and forgive, not only those around you but also yourself, that you can really begin to grow, mature and truly appreciate all that you are and can become.

Okay...now, as you sit 'still', becoming aware again of the beautiful birdsong in the background, your heart and love reaches new heights. Sound and love vibrates on many levels of consciousness as light now envelopes you, bringing peace and tranquillity to those who have drawn close to you.

Just as thunder and lightning, or an earthquake, sends waves of energy far and wide, it covers vast distances touching those by sight, sound, or sensations within. Souls that may be thousands of your earth miles away may still be touched to hear the noise, see the brightness or sense the tremors. Your heart is more powerful than all of these combined, because your heart is my heart.

If you release the truth from within your heart, your love will pour like water over rocks. In time it will erode the toughest and hardened imperfections and attitudes such as ego, jealousy, pride, and not just your own, but in many others too. Your love may trickle down at first, like a tear falling from your face, but with perseverance and effort and your appreciation of life, it will shine like the Sun and flow like the ocean, touching every shoreline and heart, and then you will be blessed with my grace.

Be kind and good to yourself and all that you are, for you will reflect this upon all things and they in turn upon you. Appreciation is a gift you can give to others and I will forever offer it to you. Believe it and share it always. Amen.

LESSON 37

RESPONSIBILITY

Welcome. I know that as you become 'still' again that you feel the peace and silence wash over you. With this, the toils of the day fade into the background and you sense the feeling of 'oneness' once again. It will always be this way, for while you are constantly aware of me in all that your senses prevail, when you dull the mind, it becomes easier to understand and realise this very fact.

Earlier today, you were thinking how beautiful and glorious the sunshine was and how the blue sky made all seem bright and wonderful, just like the 'hymn and song'. (The words shine out the essence of joy in all that is around you). People feel alive and happy when the feeling of peace and tranquillity encompasses their thoughts and senses. Well, let us continue with this theme in today's lesson or passage of learning to help reduce one's yearning.

As you all go about your daily rituals; be it work, rest or play, you can either comprehend so much more of what is within you and around you or you can become oblivious, as if on 'auto-pilot'.

That said, if one proceeds through the day without any awareness of who they are or what they are doing... is it because they do not need to think? Is each day a repetition? Is it a daily grind? If you are going through the motions can you make the switch towards taking control of your destiny?

Circumstances in and around every Soul can be deemed as perpetual joy or an ever-increasing angst of worry, fear and stress. Of whose perception would it be if your situation was either of those scenarios?

Always, you can alter how you feel in everything that occurs within your days, weeks, months, or years. The secret is for you to become detached from whether you 'think' something is good or bad, lucky or unlucky, a gift or a sacrifice and so on.

It would help if you can then realise that everything does not occur with a double-headed coin, a pre-ordained win or lose. A true coin with a head and a tail, a positive and a negative reveals not only truth but is fair and simple because they are just a reflection of each other. Again, the key to utilising the secret that is beginning to rise up within you is your own perception and no one else's.

I am not suggesting that you discount or ignore what you see, hear or touch and in what you experience through thought, word and deed. Rather you, as the individual take a responsibility for your own development and educational path.

As explained before, no other Soul can erase or balance any karma that another carries. (However, love can assist and guide when and wherever it is required to do so).The simple analogy is that you can lead a horse to water but you cannot make it drink, will also suffice here.

So, how can this responsibility become accepted by the individual or the majority? Will it be with disdain or anger and fear? Perhaps people will overcome any potential trepidation they may have, to realise that these are all false concerns and should actually be deemed as smaller, irritating inconveniencies instead.

This is much easier when you consider that during their acknowledgment, the genuine comprehension of the aim is grasped and self-realisation becomes second nature. All negativity is left behind in your shadow as you continue to walk in and towards the light, and live in love and truth.

Each day is a new opportunity to shine, no matter your age, health or wealth. You could be an infant or a great grandparent and the sun that shines upon your face is the same. You sense and feel its warmth the same way. Likewise, no matter what colour your skin, you will still feel the cold or the heat depending on the layers of the clothes you wear.

In the same way, if you lay your head down upon a soft pillow or a hard rock, it will depend upon your inner character if one perceives it as blessing or a burden. In the acceptance of any situation you should shine as brightly as you can. Always your reaction to all events can be felt by those who are around you, both seen or unseen.

Energy both within and out transmutes and transcends positive and negative feelings, thoughts and actions near and far. These can help others, both human or of a vast array of 'beings', or they can do the opposite to hinder and counteract love, light, and truth.

In realising such, it should be easier to understand the 'resonance' of all that you do has an effect on many levels of your life and those whom you come into contact with. As stated earlier, the choices are yours for the responsibility is for yourself and your 'self' is you.

Do not be daunted by such reasoning, and remember I am you and you are me. Always, the power and love is within you to overcome any obstacle that your path takes. It is this promise that erases fear in life of so called death....which is the illusion that billions still carry around in their minds after more than two thousand of your earth years have passed.

I can describe or tell you millions and millions of different things. I can also show you the 'glory' of me, but it is always down to yourself whether you wish to truly 'see'. By opening your heart, Soul, and mind as 'one' (not three) you will gain true insight that will lead and carry you forward into eternity.

Accepting another way to assist your thinking and believing can always be found in a 'youthfulness' regarding all spiritual matters. Just like your physical form which grows older and hopefully more mature, it is also wise to recall and remember the essence and fruitfulness of youth.

There lies a belief in freedom and creativity that is often suppressed as your life changes and family ties and responsibilities take hold. Again, it is perception and closure of the mind that inhibits ideas of freedom, peace and the one real choice that matters to all of you.

Your perceptions and reactions to every minute of your existence help to determine so very much in your lives. Do you see good or evil? Do you trust or mistrust? Do you fear or conquer fear? Do you love or let love pass you by? Do you give or do you take? Do you share or even care?

I know exactly what every Soul, mind and heart is, was and shall be so I do not need the answers for any questions like the above. They are only asked so that you question your own conscience and feelings, as you sleep or when you are awake. It is down to you all whether to accept or deny what matters, or if you're current embodiment can really understand what love is.

Again, I state that you all have a unique opportunity to grasp and clear so very much of what has been holding you back in this lifetime. My responsibility in loving you and guiding you will never diminish and I am forever within and by your side.

Your responsibility is to yourself (first and foremost) in terms of your own spiritual education. You can read volumes and volumes of text and view a multitude of pictures, but it is in your character, attitude, and deeds that can help wipe the slate clean.

In your youth and prime you are all more carefree. By the very same token, by caring for yourself and for all living things in the name of truth, you will set yourself free. I urge you to change from the 'talk the walk' to 'walk the talk'. Every Soul can set an example to another and this is a shared responsibility of you all. Amen.

LESSON 38

MERCY

I am here as always and know all circumstances and the reasoning behind your thoughts, words and deeds. Many can be oblivious to all or any of the above, or they can recognise me in everything that is seen or unseen, felt or sensed, both from within and out.

In your daily lives, minute by minute, hour by hour, your tasks and events unfurl before you. Your mind thinks and tries to anticipate the actions you commit or of those who are around you at any given time.

You also believe that you are in control of most situations or when in contact with fellow human beings, animals or even numerous energies in different times, dimensions and planes of existence.

It is most people's practice to strive and strive to achieve something in their lives and again the belief that it is always their actions that bring about 'results'. This can lead to pushing oneself to the limit or even punishing oneself if the 'goal' is unattained.

Most would benefit in realising that it is in the letting go of any hardened attitudes and such beliefs that leads to one gaining strength and true fulfilment. Know that I can hear, see and, above all, know you better than you can ever know yourself.

If and when you become weak or despair that you have in some way let me down, understand that my mercy will bless you and fill you with grace. Do not feel that you fail me, but rather think and believe that in comprehending your times of weakness, I am with you and will make you even stronger.

Negative actions or thoughts can haunt the individual or the masses, and it will irritate and pick at you when you feel low, inadequate, unworthy, disillusioned, or weak. Even the hearts of those who are retired or elderly and who have more life experience upon the 'Earth plane' than most, can let boredom and frustration become host to these feelings, thoughts and actions.

However, mercy can counteract all such traits and will turn them around to become their exact opposite. Mercy can fulfil you and ignite your enthusiasm, so that if and when those periods of your life which become intolerable, unbearable, and all consuming, you will know in your heart that Divine intervention has taken place.

Upon numerous occasions there are windows of opportunity to accept

119

mercy or to deny it to others. You can be gentle and caring or be controlling, and this will project false ego upon another.

Every day of you life you will have the choices appear in front of you. It is then for the individual and the individual alone to either embrace and protect their personality and character, whilst being illumined with true human values, or to succumb to lower energies and traits of a beast or zombie-like being.

When you accept mercy within you life, then this new path brings you forward to see that it is a present, a golden nugget of your growth; spiritually, mentally and emotionally. This leads you on to unconditional love and drives away any last traces of fear that may linger in your heart or mind.

It also provides you with a renewed hope and vigour, to achieve those ambitions and fulfil the dreams that you strive to embark upon. Remember, it is only the dream from within that will lead you to the true 'treasure' at the end of the rainbow.

You may believe on many occasions that the world is turning against you in a variety of complex ways. You may also feel that you didn't get that job you wanted, that house move, a relocation didn't proceed and too many other instances to mention.

There may be countless conflicts and disagreements that lead you upon new or different directions from your intended route. Instead of negative thoughts and perhaps feeling out of control or pressured by your conscious mind, an alternative to this could be that they are the set of consequences that provide the precise moment that you need to move on and flourish as a person and as a Soul. Again, it can be in the letting go, or in the non-doing, that triggers your destiny and path to self-realization and fulfilment.

So, where do you go from here? During your work, rest, or play, do you let mercy fill your hearts? Do you then share and act with that same merciful appreciation of a true love for all, or does some hidden selfishness rear its head?

Please understand that these words written are for your guidance only. I do not make commandments or rules that inhibit or punish you on pain of so-called death. If I could desire, then my desire would be that you recognise the innate truth of your being and that, as such, everything would fall into place in an instant.

Throughout all dimensions, not only has there been this inner conflict between people, beings, and animals, but also between nations of the Earth and right across galaxies and solar systems throughout time and space. In them all it is the lack of mercy in the Soul that has delayed or prevented individual or mass Ascension.

This is because of the imbalance and negative karma that escalates on a massive scale, touching many a life and heart. So, what does it take for someone who feels this to stop and realise their actions and the consequences of cause and effect?

Do they see the tears that fall? Do they hear the screams of pain from the body or heart? Some, who feel that they are in charge, do not, being oblivious to it all. Unless a realization that mercy is needed and also bestowed upon them, then it is unlikely that this will be reflected outwardly from within. Like all opportunities, they must be acted or spoken with truth. If this is not taken up, then the result is merciless and meaningless.

Likewise, in some religious beliefs upon the 'Earth plane' there are those who deviate and twist the truth for their own gains. Often it is to seek power or notoriety and, in one moment preach that I am peace and love and that "God is great", while the next moment, they will shoot and kill another human being or animal, without mercy.

It is during these troubled times that you should remain optimistic, positive and courageous in your belief system and religion. No matter what your colour, race or nationality, kindness, peace, goodwill, compassion and mercy need to prevail. All must eventually draw together and realise that there is only one religion and that is the religion of love.

By all means, wherever you are reborn onto the 'Earth plane', practise the faith of your forbears and your nation. Be proud of this and of your heritage, wherever it leads you in truth.

On all paths and upon all roads your destination is the same, returning to fulfil your true goal and live as 'one' forever. In every aspect of your own individual journeys, have and wear mercy upon your sleeve and also keep it safe within your heart.

With my grace, I bless and share my mercy with you all, which in turn you will know in every aspect of your being. Be true in all you say and do. If you are weak, acknowledge it and move on. Do not dwell upon the past. Try to forgive others and just as importantly, yourself.

If you live in truth, then you cannot fear. If you dispel fear, then you will know I am near. When you know I am near, then you will hear. Then, when you hear me you will know me. In knowing me you will find your true self, a living flame born from a spark, which glows eternal and shines mercifully from our 'one' true heart. Amen.

LESSON 39

SPIRITUAL EDUCATION AND MEMORY

Welcome again. In the past several years we have discussed information regarding the title above and how, within the physical, your memory is so important. Indeed, as soon as you're physical embodiment becomes apparent to you, all you see, hear, touch, taste, and feel becomes imprinted deep within your psyche.

However, as most know, memory (and the loss of it) greatly affects those around you, often in a very dramatic and emotional way too. Today, we will not dwell on how these actually effect your earthbound situation of work, rest, and play, but moreover, how this asset of 'remembering' is in both the Soul and your heart.

So many people ask about the connection between the physical and spiritual worlds, but this implies a division or separation, which of course there isn't for everything is whole. Likewise, when one talks about the ability to recall events from which the 'senses' have experienced; they can be mistaken as occurrences only effecting that individual. Of course this is not the case and this will become more apparent as your true knowledge, wisdom and self-realisation takes hold.

So, to start with, after physical rebirth, you are immediately 'learning' in the bodily form. As you grow and attend infant, junior, senior school and perhaps even college or university, you continue to develop your acquisition of information helping you to achieve desired objectives in your life. Later, your decisions that were made during those years then help you to start employment and so forth.

A well-known phrase of 'you never stop learning' is most appropriate because whatever you do in life, no one can profess to know or do everything and also have every ability going too. Some may continue an earthbound education well into their adulthood and also way into their advanced years too. Again, a phrase, 'you're never too old to learn' comes to forefront of most people's minds.

Well now I require you to turn your thought process to one of 'spiritual' education because if one adheres to truth, everything, yes, everything falls into place. Your memory of your Soul and heart shines like a beacon to me. I know your karma, your thoughts, words and deeds and all there is to know about every Soul. As we are 'one' I know you as I know myself.

I Am I: The In-Dweller of Your Heart

Your task and 'goal' as beings of 'Love and Light' is to be illuminated by bliss. Your memory of (many) incarnations is imprinted within you and is many, many times more detailed than your physical DNA. Your experiences and lifetimes, like markers within your history, display hope and peace, goodwill or death, darkness and decay. These are both sides of the same coin and your karma plays out, no matter when, where or how old you are.

Your 'spiritual' education throughout your lifetimes could be immense or it could be infinitesimal because it is you, your Soul, who either strives or denies itself the truth. You have noted before that upon 'crossing over' into the light after your physical death (when it is appropriate), your Soul decides for itself that it will return to the physical and continue to learn and balance karma.

Only when self-realisation becomes integrated into every aspect of your being, do you ascend into your permanent state to where you truly belong. One cannot force or speed this along by taking one's own physical life. Whatever memory or karmic imbalance has yet to come into play will have to be acted out at some point as there is no escape from cause and effect. That said, it is vital that you comprehend the following information; for during each and every single human being's lifetime an opportunity knocks.

Many a play on words could be stated here, such as a 'get out of jail free card' and 'take a chance'. I will not say that your karmic imbalance will be erased in an instant, but explain that you all have a unique and wonderful opportunity to achieve your true dream. I ask that each Soul opens their heart right now...today, not tomorrow, next week, next month, or year.

You do not need a library of text to decipher the true imprint of love within and upon your heart. You do not need to disappear from view and sink into total solitude to find me. You do not need to be a martyr to any belief or false declaration. Simply this, remember, yes <u>remember,</u> who and what you truly are!

Do not mistake the physical as me, for you were not 'created' in my image this way. The cloud of illusion deceives, but you can blow this away with one breath of hope, faith and love which you already are and always will be. Your Soul and heart cannot die or fade to grey, for you are 'life' more colourful than crystals and rainbows and more beautiful than your minds can ever imagine.

Realise your memory is like an internal clock; it keeps ticking away, does not stop and spiritually cannot reverse. Therefore, using it to your advantage you can grow steadily, patiently, lovingly and develop into a caring human being that in serving society, serves me, thus serving yourself.

I Am I: The In-Dweller of Your Heart

As your 'spiritual' education grows and you become at peace in all you do, so you're imbalanced karma can be erased. Those sticky black molasses of deceit, hate, greed, jealousy, and so forth will be dissolved around your light and the radiating coil of your heart, which then shines infinitely brighter day by day. As said, you can achieve your destiny in this lifetime. Do you want to take that chance? Are you willing to take that chance?

Barriers that you yourself have erected can be broken away. Your love, power and heart know no bounds, so nothing is holding you back. You can achieve everything and anything and by staying focused on your true goal you can escape what you yourself have created over many millennia.

Know this, I will never leave you. I will carry you and help you. Take one step to me and I will move many more to thee. One day you will be home, I promise you. Discover the truth always 'within', for you will know beauty beyond all things; it is no mystery, as there is only **you**. Amen.

LESSON 40

FAMILY AND THE TREE OF LIFE

We begin your notes today with the title above. Some may think that these are separate issues, however they are very much entwined, for both form a basis for growth and expansion in so many ways.

When someone wishes to investigate their heritage, they will ask close relatives for information. Furthermore, they'll look at history, its records and publications, to form what you know as the family 'tree'.

Straight away you can sense the collaboration and the connection with each other. On occasions people can trace through factual evidence of where and what family members were doing and also why. The birth, death and marriage details all lead and leave a trail of those who were close (or distant) from you over hundreds if not thousands of years.

In addition to this historic information of documents and photographs you also have DNA links that are handed down from generation to generation. In essence all are linked. Every being, both human as well as the vast array of intelligent life that exists within and on different vibration levels, are all connected in some way.

People could say though that if they don't physically see something, (suggesting that they need some 'hard' evidence) then it does not exist or it isn't true. In time truth will clear all the illusions and confusion that cloud minds and hearts and this will empower them to fulfil their goal, returning to bliss and true peace in me. So, one may discover next of kin such as aunts, uncles, cousins, nephews and so forth and many more that they hadn't realised existed.

How would this make one feel? Indifferent, concerned, wondering in anticipation, or perhaps disinterested even? A voyage of discovery could cease at this point or it could be pursued and delved into much deeper. Perhaps a yearning or an obsession to find out where one belongs or where you fit in could become more important.

I discuss this point of view as you take in its reflection and another meaning, that it's your trace of your life that takes more importance at this time. The documents that can be seen and read do not explain your character and the love that lies within and is expressed by you. These are the things that are your true legacy and connection.

So your family past, present and also in the future has (or will) decide many things, not just for yourself but also having implications and consequences for many whom they come into contact with. Here we can divert into karmic 'inheritance' and also to continue the family thread. You should now be comprehending 'family of the Soul' or your 'Soul's family'.

Through your numerous embodiments over the passage of time, (which is due to the imbalance of your heart) Souls are joined and form bonds of love that cannot break. In one lifetime you could have been a mother or father to one of your parents. That sibling could have been your husband or wife in another lifetime and so on.

This may sound bizarre but it is simple and straight forward and also of and for the karmic balancing to be undertaken by all who require it. This doesn't always happen but it is a process and link to each other that needs to be conveyed.

Ok, now consider that all participate and form a 'tree of life'. Think of this as one simple structure, but also now know of the power and how magnificent it is. The tree of life is 'I', for all things are from, through and to me. This explains that nothing is separate or different, below or above or inside or out of me.

Consider the roots of a tree, it anchors it in its location and is the foundation for its life. It can grow strong and tall as roots are embedded deep within the soil. Likewise your histories of many lifetimes are the roots of your Soul.

The trunk of the tree shoots upwards, it reaches towards the 'heavens' and the sunlight and warmth help it grow. So too, the light of the Lord who is the 'witness' sustains you and helps you too know yourself. The Lord has no attachment to anything, yet as we are all one, you live in him and I live in you.

The tree grows from and to the light and so do you. You should strive to be the best person and Soul you can be. By focusing on the light you will eradicate negativity, darkness and decay in all that you think, say, and do.

From the trunk grows branches like strong arms that weave within the wind. The branches have shoots that grow, expanding it to reach further into its surroundings. Your family are like a branch of the living tree and the shoots that grow are the siblings. All are connected and all are one.

Sometimes branches become too heavy or old, sometimes the offshoots in their tenderness snap and fall away. Do not despair, for as they lay on the ground they are then journeying back through the roots and source of all things and life. Some Souls realise this quickly while others take a long time to remember.

Know that by gazing upon a tree in its different seasons you can understand a simple process. After the winter time of your sleeping years being in denial, realise through truth you gradually awaken again. A time will come when spring alerts you to the splendour of Creation and the blossoming of your love.

Recognition arrives as love and light radiates from and through you. The tree's leaves are returning and they form a canopy, a crown of beauty and elegance that both protects and captivates. Wisdom and knowledge and understanding then filter through to the branches of you all. The giver of all life knows exactly what each and every one need and exactly 'when' too.

Summer arrives and you bask in the glory and the splendour which you can feel every day if you choose too. The core of life is love and you are all part of me. Do not think of those that are near the top of the tree as any better than you. Ego has no importance, so strive to be 'you' and live in truth.

When you are ready it is time to return to your permanent state and those leaves in autumn will fall. You will return to bliss and peace that is your true inheritance. My breath will blow the leaves so watch them fly and soar so high. My love will guide you all, every single one, straight back home to me. Amen.

LESSON 41

OASIS

When you become quiet and 'still' you can feel my presence. The peace and tranquillity and the love that is I, impresses upon your earthly senses, but most importantly it is felt within your heart and Soul. Your everlasting light that sparkles brighter through, from and to me shines eternal and in truth no amount of darkness, decay or negativity can ever erase who and what you are.

I know you all, the countless billions upon many worlds and civilizations throughout all time and in all places. No distance, separation and amount of time can detract or take any one of you away from me. I am the breath that you inhale and I am your heart that beats and pumps your life's energy in all the bodies that you have possessed in the past, present and, if required, the future too.

Likewise, you're mental, emotional, physical and astral bodies flow within, from and travel to me also. Your current journey, you call 'this lifetime' is but a click of a finger and passes through the eons of time almost unnoticed. Some would say and reflect that perhaps it means that they have gone by without achievement or recognition of any kind; however I do not mean this.

Imagine for a moment a grain of sand on a beach, minute and almost invisible to the naked eye, but cup your hands together and you will find millions of grains that flow through your fingertips. Each one is alone but not alone, for together they are whole.

By being 'together' much is achieved. Results may not be shown in your physical world, but in essence combined hearts with unconditional love achieve great and wonderful things. Some aren't seen or heard, but acts of compassion and kindness reverberate beyond physical walls. They cascade like water over rocks, wearing away hardened attitudes and stubborn 'character' to lift and heal deep within. These are the true achievements that people should give back to society.

So, the life that has manifested itself with your karma and inherited action may appear long and fruitful in its bodily cloth that you wear, but exterior beauty is, was, and always will be a minute part of your Soul's history.

As your physical body becomes tired and worn, due to its impermanent state, the time will come when it can no longer function. As your Spirit drifts into light, 'recognition' will befall those who have not believed or remembered that they are all things.

Upon their recall of this understanding, the mind will know all that they have ever been. The energy spiralling with coherent intellect and wisdom of many a lifetimes, cause and effect will imprint upon the Soul and they will then realize their goal and true destiny.

I explain this because so many still do not comprehend the light that they are. Earthbound days of work, rest and play seemingly fill every waking minute and this leaves little time for contemplation, peace and stillness.

The life you have can be a happy one, even in the direst of situations and events. Do not be frightened or live a life of fear. Instead, rise above negativity and anguish and therefore share your love and goodwill.

The illusion that manifests itself is like a mirage, deceiving you to believe in untruths Imagine for a moment that you are in a desert, your throat sore and dry, the heat bears down upon your every step which becomes harder and your balance more impaired. You're about to faint and your eyes becoming blurred as suddenly something appears on the horizon.

In this moment you have a decision to make, are you witnessing the truth? In front of you now is an amazing sight, palm trees are standing tall and strong encircling a crystal clear pool of water. There are flowers and plants of every colour capturing the sun and blooming in radiance and glory. You fall to your knees and ask yourself, are they real, or are they all false?

Of course, now you would like an answer wouldn't you? Well, perhaps there is more to this than meets the eye. Here you must think and ponder. Here you must decide for yourself. In all that you have read and learnt and digested in your lifetime, do you believe in what you see or in what you feel? Is it one, the other or both? Is it a question of faith? Do you trust in yourself? If you do then you trust in me.

When and if you experience the uncertainty, doubt or the fear that is falsely captivating you I say this, do not be afraid, and know that your heart and Soul are true. Do not think you are alone, for you can never be. Should times be hard for whatever reason, I am with you. I love you and I will stay with you into the known or unknown. If you thirst I will be the water upon your lips. If you cry, I will be the hand that wipes your tears away.

Some days you may think your heart is breaking into two, but I am the love that will heal and mend, and my light is magical 'glue'. When your joy is too much to withhold, your laughter strong and loud, the echo of such happiness I will send far beyond earthly clouds. Every minute, hour, day, week, or year I ask only that your heart opens wider to 'hear' the true voice that's deep inside, which is a reflection of your Soul.

I Am I: The In-Dweller of Your Heart

Behold and cast out doubt, for love and bliss will lead you unto your goal. So cast aside illusions of the misty blurred mirage and see the true oasis of Love that I am, for I will save all hearts. Do not be dismayed when you think I ignore your calls, for justice and its scales watch over all, even if you stumble or fall.

When you are ready to embark upon 'light's' journey, all will be revealed as you Ascend into what is past the 'heavenly'. Then with layers of love and peace I will place a coat of many colours upon thee and to all around, for one and all your hearts, they are truly bound.

Always we are together in light and every sound, with my heart forever open and in you all, I am so proud. Vibrations they'll come and go, but in love there is no end. 'One' we'll always be, into eternity you and me. Amen.

LESSON 42

DREAMS AND VISIONS

I am here and have waited for you to commence writing David. Your day's toils are over, tasks completed and now it's your time and 'our' time to feel and think as 'one' which of course you already are.

As your heart starts to relax and slow down, its beat now falls to a slower and gentler rhythm. Your mind is becoming free once more, rather than filled with issues and matters of the impermanent and physical world.

Stillness washes over you and also the many that now also draw in close to you. They too are waiting to learn and digest the 'truth' on their own path and journey. Then in time, what is gained is then shared freely and wisely with love and kindness so that others too can then grow and mature at the level they have reached.

At this precise moment, as these words enter your mind and heart, there will be those who also think that you communicate with the 'dead'. These thoughts and phrases still complicate matters and the issue at hand is that many beings in numerous dimensions still believe that the physical Universe is all that there is.

It will remain difficult for those with these view-points, until their hearts and minds expand to be infused with the truth that each individual Soul needs to shatter its own illusions and confusion. It often seems that no single instance or example of love and light that shines through is enough.

Whilst I describe this, I must make it clear that I do not become angry or frustrated with any elements of life when these situations occur. Rather, I sense (not feel) sadness reflected towards and through me, for while I am all things, the love which can be as complex or as simple as anyone can make it, will touch me in all ways; always.

So, those who now encompass you come from many levels of learning and through many levels of vibration-energy. Elements of light and 'life' can travel distance and time in the blink of an eye, whilst there are those who are here by thought or through their heart's centre at this very moment.

Why do they come to link like this? They do so for progress, sometimes for themselves, but often for next of kin, brethren or for those who live in shadow or darkness. What is learnt is then passed on in numerous ways.

Assistance to human beings, animals and creatures that man could not

131

even conceive, as well as energies and life forces that your minds would fear can happen physically, emotionally and mentally, as well as at different levels of the psyche.

Over the years you have yourself documented many of your dreams and visions, some precognitive. As you know, your sleep is not just for your physical recuperation, but is also gives 'Spirit', your guides and teachers an opportunity to help and assist you.

Throughout history upon the earth many people were called or deemed to be witches, soothsayers, or clairvoyants as well as devil worshippers, charlatans and frauds. Notable names such as Nostradamus and Joan of Arc are but two who you could state had the gift of foresight. It is often for the educational purpose of their soul that this inherent ability (that is in all life) was able to be expressed this way.

You yourself, through thought and prayer many years ago, asked for proof and for help to grow. I do not deny anything or any ability to anyone and if you believe and you are sincere and hope with all your heart, then dreams can come true.

However, it is also very important to remember that karma has its role to play and the balance of whom and what is around both the individual and the masses is also significant in this aspect.

So, as billions of beings sleep, what exactly is happening? Scientists, philosophers and many well noted names, past and present, such as Plato, Jung and Freud, have all documented the vast variety of attributes of the brain and mind. Today though, it is not appropriate to delve into topics and areas such as alpha and beta waves, impulses, vortex's, unconsciousness, and the like.

What is required at all times of Spiritual education is simplicity, as love, light and truth are all simple in their constitution and are needed in all thoughts, words and deeds of life.

Often people wake from sleep with dreams that are bizarre and frightening, or calming, emotional and heart-warming, or even spiritual and visionary. Some resemble what the person enacted during their day or become a reflection of what had occurred yesterday, last week, last year, or even right back to childhood.

Whilst many trained professionals may discount images or feelings that come to someone's mind as trivial and unimportant, I explain that it is for the individual only to come to that conclusion.

One can have dreams analysed and separated into pigeon-holes of expression, but it should be remembered that the dream is for the individual only. No two dreams are alike, even if they are believed to be, just as two flowers of the same variety can ever be the same.

I Am I: The In-Dweller of Your Heart

Dreams are a release and also a source of learning from deep within your Soul. They can be memorable or they can disappear as if without a trace, leaving a person to wonder; 'What was it for?' Just as all thoughts, both positive and negative, have a cause and effect, so do dreams. They can always remain as insignificant or as important as that person deems. Nothing is ever wasted and therefore there is always an impression upon the dreamer, no matter how small it can be.

Spiritual or educational dreams will light up and stand out significantly from the rest. These can assist you in your daily lives and by taking notice of them you can become more of a recipient to new avenues of Soul growth and awareness.

People often have visions, or recall magical moments of illumination that lay deep within their hearts. These can also come from the Soul (and Soul connections) to the love and light all around them and also to and from Spiritual guides and teachers. This process has helped you yourself, David, to be where you are today in terms of understanding, knowledge, and wisdom and so you are 'living' proof (if this was required), that this is true and the case.

Remember that <u>any</u> guidance, whether it is by day or night, if you are awake or asleep must be the truth, in truth and from truth. It is your own responsibility as per any Soul to question whether any information or guidance is given in the name of love, light and truth.

It doesn't matter if someone hears, sees, touches, or tastes and digests through the body, mind, or Soul (three but all 'one'), for it will always resonate deep within. It is right for that individual, if it feels right. No source of truth will ever be frustrated or angry if he, she, they, or 'it' is then asked whether what is given comes in my name and in or from 'love'.

Remember, too, that millions of creatures and beings also roam the many vibration energies and dimensions by day and by night, within light and darkness. Do not ever fear of what I tell and explain here to you, as I have stated countless times that you are not, and can never be, alone. I am you and you are me.

Your dreams and visions are known to me before they even happen. They occur through, to and from me and as such all that you will ever sense and feel is ultimately my experience too.

As the many now prepare to leave this gathering and have shared the love of 'one' heart, know that you are my greatest gift and expression. Whilst you're awake or asleep and drifting through my love, we are attached and inseparable and remain one forever. Every dream and vision that can ever be 'realised' and experienced, both through and by you, also returns to me. It is the present (gift) that I have pre-sent within this present time that

133

you should always learn to treasure. Amen.

LESSON 43

MYSTERIES

Be still and feel my peace and comfort as it protects and lifts your consciousness to greater and brighter things. When you are still it enables the individual to be their true self and to reflect, like a mirror, the radiance of Love and Light that you are.

During times of quietness, peace will wrap around you like a layer of finest silk that cannot be seen or touched by human senses. None the less, it is there as a token of my affection to and for you all.

When you disconnect the exterior thoughts, concerns, and the illusion of any fears that you have, then you become a being that can truly comprehend and understand who, what and why you are to go 'beyond' the place in the world that you now reside.

Often people feel trapped in their own demise when in reality you are all free. But how can this be so when your home, environment, family, work, etcetera is spun like a web all around you? Perhaps you could picture the hub of a wheel instead, with the spokes leading out to the circle which contains you. This could lead to thoughts that, without you to connect to everything, all those around you whom you feel depend upon your existence, will fall down and fail to exist.

Instead of these images that now flash through your mind, imagine the hub as your heart and Soul and the spokes as rays of your Love and Light that emanate in all directions. It is this that truly exists and nourishes those around you physically, mentally, emotionally and within the ethereal realms of existence. This is more important to get right rather than the material aspects of the world around you.

Now then, as your very core finds rest, do not let exterior feelings or thoughts enter your being. These will only restrict your ability to truly see with your eyes of mind, body and Soul as one. They are not separate and so true insight prevails.

In this state you can find all the answers you seek and it is this that needs nurturing and rekindling to ignite the spark within. When your flame burns brightly it illuminates into the darkness and erases internal and external negativity, worries and stress enabling you to feel your correct path and true self and goal. Eventually, understanding and wisdom ensues, leading to self-realization and eternal bliss in me.

Until human beings fully know themselves, then the level of true intellect and the comprehension of many mysteries remain. Throughout time immemorial scholars and sages, together with scientists and religions, have disagreed on many areas of discovery and the information collected. One looks for answers, but more often than not they are sought incorrectly.

As discussed once before, mankind still looks for information externally rather than internally. Many have found clues for what they are looking for when they are not actually seeking the answer itself. Flashes of inspiration and 'Eureka' moments describe what I mean.

This is because truth is relayed when and where it is needed and at the correct time for progress' sake. Please do not fret or misunderstand, nothing is held purposefully back if it is for the benefit of the individual and their circumstance of the expansion of Love and Light.

Within your current state of technology and its search for understanding of such things like Space and the Universe, these just keep revealing more questions than answers. Beyond the Earth, your satellites and communications are sent to discover and examine planets, moons, the solar system, and so forth. You look to evaluate the 'big bang' and contemplate 'dark matter' and dark energy and the effects and meanings of such occurrences.

Scientific minds across the globe wonder in amazement at such things and some hope that answers they find will help their fellow man. Please, do not misunderstand that inspiration and information can help you all, but ultimately it would be of greater help for your wellbeing as a human race to live and love each other.

Discovery and the searching of many a mind is not at all wrong, but it is sad that millions go hungry or live in poverty when the worlds community could share so much of its wealth and power to live and radiate Love and Light. (Now that would be true progress!) However, great minds such as Einstein and Galileo wanted and needed to expand both to grow and discover, so many scientists and astronomers are no different today.

Having mentioned 'dark matter' and 'dark energy' a few of your moments ago, let me clarify a so-called mystery. These both go hand in hand. It is true that the Universe is expanding and hence in millions of your Earth years as distances between worlds extend, planets will freeze, composite structures will change or evolve differently.

Intellectual minds though will state they want specifics, equations, information and the like, but they are not ready. All must strive (if that is their academic goal) to discover the truth. As we are all 'one' and I am everything, so you are everything too. The pulses and the contracting and expanding of matter are the essence felt of my heat-beat and also of my breath. Do not picture a human heart, but try to imagine a source and power of all things instead.

All the billions of galaxies and solar systems are a minute part of me. That said, people will now say that mankind must be infinitesimal, or even insignificant. No, because of your essence, your heart and Soul, you are all things too. You are me and I am you. No division… wholeness. This is why you can know everything that your 'need' requires if in truth, Love and Light.

So, be positive and kind in your actions, thoughts and words. Hold dear your faith in yourself, for then your faith in me is sustained. Do not forget me, but hold me close in all your endeavours. Do not be afraid or fear will eat away your conscience and the ability to live in harmony and peace.

You can all try to learn and question that which is far beyond the Earth, but ultimately your most direct route to me is not the exterior but the interior. There lies your greatest mystery and the most beautiful discovery and answer. I am willing you and I am waiting for you. Know yourself and you will know me, I love and care for you all. Amen.

LESSON 44

NATURE

Welcome. As I am closer than near, I know when you are 'still' and ready to receive the next lesson. As a child waits for the teacher to begin, they must be prepared and ready to open their heart and mind in order that what is shown or spoken is received without barriers of the exterior illusion and confusion we have discussed so often before.

Being 'still' confirms that a process is taking place, both within and out, for both energies and vibration levels of light resonate at the same pitch, bringing the abilities that you possess to the surface of self; illuminating, and shining in all directions.

Once this occurs, many beings, both spiritual and ethereal, can link and combine with the resulting connections taking place. A knock-on effect transpires to alleviate the recipient's blockages in their chakras, thus enabling them to receive higher energies that resonate and pulse at greater speeds than at which their physical currently resides.

I explain this to you now as many, many, Souls have drawn close to you this 'evening'. You may or may not sense them, but this is not a task or an issue for you at this time or in this process either.

The important thing is the effort that is made to partake, participate, share and freely give the love that is communicated to you all. I am not stating nor am I concerned over the work or business side of producing these books, but wish to reflect true comparisons between you all as human beings, with what you can see and feel all around you.

Here, I am talking about the world in which you live and life upon the Earth as you currently perceive it in Nature. With information from guides and helpers on the earth, you have already noted parts of this discussion in Book 1 – Pathway, and in Book 2 – Deliverance of Love, Light and Truth. Today we will take this a step further so that those who are beginning to open their true selves to Love and Light will go on to expand and help in truth.

This may occur in small 'baby' steps at first, as if attending a nursery school, but will then evolve and flourish into receiving 'higher' education if, and when, appropriate for the individual to do so.

Tonight, as you currently sit and gaze through the window, just as you have done on many previous occasions, leaves on the trees sway and blow about in the wind. Flowers that are in full bloom also dance in the breeze as the breath of life flows over them.

Sometimes, even at this time of your earth year, one or two fall to the ground, disappearing from view. Because your earthly senses cannot see or touch them, do they cease to exist? Of course not!

Likewise, because two lovers are miles apart or two friends are out of touch or even if a parent is separated from their child, does a connection end? Do the feelings dissipate or become diluted, fading into oblivion? No.

Many, many similarities exist between nature and 'human nature' but there are also vast differences. People may consider that these are obvious comparisons to make. If this were always the case, the world in which you reside would be a cleaner, safer, and a much brighter place to live.

All women and men have the truth and the ability to realise their true potential. Latent abilities remain suppressed and withdrawn due to loss of innocence, and the stress and decay of their thoughts, words, and deeds. The road to enlightenment, bliss and your permanent state of being can be as easy or as difficult as one can make it. The very nature of your difficulties lies not in others but in the 'self' and self-denial.

Mankind often hinders itself in the pursuit of impermanent desire and pleasure, a fleeting and transitory feeling of fulfilment. In truth they are not. Just as a leaf or flower petal falls to the ground, it soon discolours, its beauty fades away and then it becomes part of the background. It grew and died but it still 'resides'. Time passes and it will re-nourish and bloom in another form, just like your bodily incarnations over many millennia.

Your task and goal is to shine while you are currently here. It must be in truth, with love and compassion. In this embodiment you can obtain bliss and your impermanent state will be no more. Help and guidance will always be there for you all, for each and every Soul.

You, as the 'child', must take the steps yourself, just as the parent oversees their offspring to crawl, then kneel and stand before them. You must then walk towards the Love that beckons. Upon achieving this first real task, smiles, laughter and joy are beheld by all present.

I ask those that are embarking on their new path to take the first step towards me, a reflection of your true self. Do not fear, for I am within and by your side. On your road of light I will protect and guide you through your so called 'good' and 'bad' times. I will nurture you so that your light shines like a star both near and far.

Now, as the cloud and greys of shadow begin to clear in the sky, brightness and clarity beams down towards you. In this process there is a removal of doubt and despair and your life will be rich in contentment and peace.

It is important to understand that, just like nature around you; your seasons of change will be constant. You need to be adaptable, intuitive and go with the flow of your true inner feelings and thoughts. Of course, I do not mean that you should only ever consider those of your own, but rather make sure that all you do is in the name of truth and with the foresight and action of true human values.

Lastly today, I will relate what is flashing through your consciousness and thoughts. You think of nature's beauty and also of its destructive power. The 'elementals' of earth, air, water and fire magnify both beauty and also death.

In nature, forces ranging from the sublime and beautiful rainbow to the volcano's fire and brimstone, from the pure crystal water of the sea to the tornado or hurricane from 'hell'... each are all events and occurrences which evolve from what is consumed and emitted from all those that live on the impermanent earth. It is no more complicated or difficult to comprehend than that.

It has been and always will be important to try to live in peace and harmony and with gratitude of 'mother' earth and all that sustains you within the physical embodiment. By living with and within nature, you must realise that all life is 'one'. By doing so, every action has its reaction both positive and negative. Balance is a key for stability and harmony and in being 'still'; you can nurture your own true nature within. Amen.

LESSON 45

BEING 'STILL' IN A WEB OF LIFE

Welcome, once again. Know that the depths of one's heart can reveal an abyss or perhaps an amazing bliss and while you seek and search within yourself, you can grow and learn much more than you believe was ever possible. Do you desire this? Do you really wish this? Are you afraid of what you will discover of your true self?

Anxiety and being frustrated with one's goals and aspirations, and being wary of the choices you make and the resulting actions have an effect on yourself and those around you. Good, bad, or indifferent, they can and will impact upon your way and your path as well as those who are close by and those (seemingly) far away.

By thought, word, and deed, the seed is sown so it may grow to be nurtured and fulfilled. Or perhaps it can flounder, swirling inside the heart like a gust of wind with no resting place. Please know that just as roots of a tree flourish with soil and water, your strength of conviction and character can ground you and set you gently in place, where you can then reflect and be 'still'.

Being still helps one reflect, both within and out, to shine like a beacon instead of a tiny spark or ember. Please, remember that your Soul and heart are a flame, a living flame of my love and light, of such beauty and majestic brilliance that mere words cannot portray, let alone try to describe.

Many Souls and beings across many eras of history, vast planes and dimensions of time and light, have dampened their very essence through karma. I have said before, do not ever feel that time is running out, but state to you all that it is time to now rekindle the fire and expand in wisdom and knowledge.

You need to share with those who open their hearts and minds to grow and know of who, what, and why they 'are', have been, and also will become. Destiny is truth and truth is destiny. You cannot grow without the experience of being human, spiritual or mental in 'form'.

Understand that through these endeavours of many lifetimes and from many journeys of mind and heart, piece by piece, the darkness of 'ego' and the self falls away.

I Am I: The In-Dweller of Your Heart

You are all connected, by the strands of Light and Love,
For each a Soul is born, from within and up above.
So as you stretch and then you search, from both heart and then your mind,
I reveal that you're much more, than just one of a kind.

Like the spider's web vibrating, upon and in the wind,
Fragments of life are captured, but do you think then I have sinned?
Yes nourishment for one and maybe pain for one another,
Through experience that's for all, you are meant now to discover.

In the centre it connects, as the each strand then forms a line,
A web of life to live, in truth and you'll be fine.
The energy is forever and it can not be changed,
Only those who do not learn… will think it's all in vain.

Think of it right now, upon a cold and frosty morn,
It glistens and it glows, as the Sun then starts to warm.
The frozen elements cling, from the cold and dead of night,
Or a quiet pause of stillness, do you long to now take flight?

For peace and the truth, will melt all hardened thoughts,
Those captured by frames of time, that you think can then be bought.
Not by money or materialism or any Earth bound false pleasure,
The golden centre of all life is revealed as your true treasure.

So know you are not trapped, enclosed or be passed by,
For growth and understanding means, the higher you can fly.
You can now move on and glow bright as the 'Son',
Eternally live in peace, forever with me and you as 'one'.

Amen

LESSON 46

EACH A 'SUN' – WITH FREE WILL

Dear children of love and light, peace and truth remains with you, both during the day and the night. It never diminishes, never fails and never, ever stops to pause and reflect, even though many an individual thinks and believes it does.

You can never be alone, even when you rest or sleep. You can never be alone, even if you are in the deepest cavern or upon the highest mountain as your 'one', always and forever.

Life for the many is still regarded as being physical and in just living. Reflect within yourself to realise that this is a very singular and trivialising style of thought. Each of you must all develop from within, to expand your hearts, minds and your love from your Soul.

This is Universal; a love connection can never be expired or extinguished. It is everlasting, because I am love and always will be. There is no greater force or energy than Love and Light. It recognises and leads you to your understanding.

In this understanding it brings the wisdom and knowledge that you all seek. Two very different things of course, but they are connected as one, just the same.

It is when there is the division, the splitting of oneness and wholeness that the confusion and darkness rains in. However, you can defuse and block all ills and all decay, with such simplicity, and this is called love. This is not always easy in the face of provocation and confusion, but by trusting within and trusting in my love, there is nothing, absolutely nothing, that cannot be achieved.

Every task you set and every Soul that you seek does not lie beyond any hurdle or fence, only within, for you are Creation and part of the Love and Light of me. As this is so, you can tap into untold wealth, not materialism or of a coveted nature, but of the most important ingredient imaginable. The Universal life force of the Love and Light is deep within your Soul and yet is also in everything you see, feel, touch and sense.

All you have to do to 'become' is to want to belong; and by your faith and trust you can achieve those goals that inside yourself you need and seek. There is no mystery other than that created by human thoughts and actions and those misguided voices who dispel the truth.

You can diffuse this by and with positive thoughts of love, and by doing so, not only do you expand the precious light from within you, but also help those who cannot truly see.

All in time the world will know and then all can grow, those more quickly who wish to. No pressure or exterior influences can be utilised to coerce another. Someone may believe this is so, but it is denial of the truth that clouds the mind and heart.

Perhaps there is the belief that someone has been forced to behave a certain way or to do a course of action that is not of their own making. This is false truth and action. The individual can never be denied their free-will and ultimately it is their own Soul and their own light that decrees their path.

So, when someone denies or passes up on the acceptance of truth, it is from within that they have decided this. Can this be classed as right or wrong? Do not judge another, for they are their own judge and jury.

A Soul can be called upon at any time, that choice is also open to you, all of you and the decision to grow as a being of light is always your own. Thus, you can be called, but do you hear it? Can you hear the voice of love; the sweet, tender, gentle calling of the teacher and the master, both within and out?

You can turn the key which is your love, into the door of your heart to reveal everything, or you can hear this calling of truth and love and walk away.

Again, this is your own choice and desire, for it is you who are the door as well as the key. Yes, you are unique and each individual has a very real opportunity. By entering the doorway which is the pathway of love, you create the light, send the light, digest the light and you also share the light.

You can take a look and turn back or you can step further into the love to see all the truth that you could imagine. This will occur when you look with the heart, mind, body and Soul together in unison.

People may say, 'Isn't that really four ways of seeing then... or it is three ways as the body and heart must be one? Okay, yes we can deem the physical heart and body to be this way, but they are also separate, for every cell and molecule sees and feels the love and truth.

Know that the heart seats your Soul and it is your body that seats your heart. It is the heart that 'breathes' in the physical sense, but it also feels and supports your 'being,' along with your mind and your consciousness, so everything is whole and is 'one'.

By being and looking into the light of truth, it must also be asked; do you really see the truth? Well, if you were to look upon the burning sun, do you recognize its truth or do you squint and close your eyes at its brightness and its warmth?

I Am I: The In-Dweller of Your Heart

True vision will enable you to perceive with all that has been mentioned today, for when you gaze upon the Sun, not only would you be able to survey its beauty, but also its magnificent energy and patterns of love and light.

Not only does the Sun sustain you all with heat and light and life upon the Earth, it is also a beacon, a symbol of universal energy, a star and one of many, both near and far. There are countless in many galaxies and solar systems, though you can only observe these from within yourself and in truth.

The peace and love it sends is a symbol way beyond your billions of years of evolution, yet it belongs here and everywhere. It does not matter whether it is day or night, just like my love. If you do not see the Sun in the sky, do you then believe it is not there? Like the grey and dark mists of Earth's atmosphere, do they cloud your true vision? Feel this message within your heart and you will know its meaning.

I remind you that you are all part of the eternal 'Son' and of the Sun which I have explained are many. As such, you are also each a 'sun', giving out heat, light and love, so do not stay in the shade and the hidden darkness. Walk free and be free to share and illuminate your pathway ahead of you.

Guide all who are opening their eyes and hearts for the first time. Just like new born children, they may cry, but it takes no force or pain for them to 'realise' as the truth is gentle. Love is so immense and, by sharing and giving, they will see.

There is no need to push or shove, for it takes just a few words or a smile, a thought or even a prayer to help each one flower and bloom at their own recognition. It is not for you to decide, as I have mentioned many times before.

Likewise, I reiterate that you are also segments of the puzzle; a jigsaw. As you are all 'one', you form the overall picture and are therefore already complete. You need to view this as being more than one-dimensional, in what your physical eyes tell you can be seen.

Much work is done both above, below, within, and out and also wherever you go. You are never alone so live and shine out the light forever. Soar high and send out your love as always, for in truth and in my love you will never, ever fail.

Be 'still' now and at peace, until you are ready to release the light once again through the words of a loving pen. Amen.

LESSON 47

LIGHT AND SIGHT TO NEW LEVELS

You can open your eyes to look far and wide, but when you gaze upon things that are close by, you may not witness what lies deep in the distance. So, your eyes can perceive all and yet see nothing.

Clouds of illusion dull the mind and place a shield around your heart. Therefore, when those who do not (or wish not to) 'open up,' they can observe no further than the boundary that they themselves have set.

You do look through your eyes and this can reveal the truth or a tissue of lies. You can also look and see from the heart to grow and understand that you never part, or you can close your heart to the light and lose your true sight, your 'insight'.

The light can be viewed from many directions and in many ways, and yet it can only be recognised and understood with love. For love is the power and is the bond of radiance and Divine energy that nourishes and sustains you and your Soul.

The light emanates from me, for I am light. Yet why can all not truly see this? It is because the eyes of the mind, body and Soul are not functioning as one and just like the blurriness of misted lenses, (seeing only with and through the physical), you search through the clouds and the dullness to only find illusion. It is when you cleanse the lens of your heart, the centre of your being and Soul, that the mist can be wiped away and the truth revealed.

The way to do this is not new or only for the few. The ability to feel, grow and be encompassed by the light everlasting is there with you all. This has always been the way and it will last for eternity for those who choose to open up and reveal their true selves to the light. Yes, light to light, an open door which lies ajar and is never far. It is within you, within you all.

You do not have to look beyond the horizon and you do not have to climb the highest mountain. You do not need to cross the deepest sea or widest land to find my loving hand, as it is outstretched for each and every one of you, already! Look and you shall find. Look and you will 'ascend', as can all humankind.

The message or lesson today, from the truth and light, is for you to open up and feel, touch, taste, smell, hear, and be in the light. Yes, be in the light, for you are light, and so do not wear darkened bands around the eyes of your true self.

146

I Am I: The In-Dweller of Your Heart

Cast aside the shadows of doubt to walk and grasp the hands of light that are there for you all, for they are all around you too, in every direction, both without and 'within'.

Also cast out those feelings of hate and sin to truly open and go and begin. The love, light, truth and sight is yours to behold and the vision to win. Yes, to win the right to eternity in the light. It is yours to take, but what is at stake? It is the need(s) to live, learn and sometimes yearn, both for the peace and love that you all seek to find.

So then, understand that you are me and I am you, and together we are all one of a kind. Remember, you are each a 'wing', a part of the dove of peace. Love is the partner and the key, for it enables you to take flight, to fulfil your destiny, your true insight. Fly high, as high as you might both every day and every night. Just seek the truth in all you do, then all your dreams, they will come true.

The musical notes that flow, above you and below,
They move like many Souls, but which way do they go?
They sing and also chime, in the peace of the Divine,
Or do they drift into the mist, forever and for all time?

A search truly begins, when the door it has been opened,
To lead you all in to, bestow not be broken.
A reward for those who have, revealed unto themselves,
That life is for love and knowing, the 'I' and then the self.

Inside of you is light and you're so welcome please don't hide,
Eternal life is for each and all, to take up and on this ride.
Towards Ascension and a level, of love and joy …no pain,
Are sacrifice and your task, forever all in vain?

In truth so do not worry, for you are overseen,
To pastures rich and new or before where you have been.
There is something true, in every voice and smile and thing,
But revealed is it now only, by pure hearts now out of sin?

So the choice is truth, and yours alone to make,
And in the peace you ask: 'But what is it at stake?'
Only you can then define, where your goal and path is set,
But for me you were not born, as we've already met.

I Am I: The In-Dweller of Your Heart

And from the burning Sun, you're everlasting in my love,
Do not ask of where you're from; below or up above?
Because it's only just and just it only is,
No need to ever worry, a Soul's choice is one for bliss.

As the rays fall from within and also then without,
Please do not ever cry, or plead or cast a doubt.
Because the goodness you each do, will see you then all through,
For this love contains it 'all'…and includes both me and you.

Then you'll see the 'Son', and ask of the why, the how and when,
Open hand to now just write, with love and I deep through this pen.
You can go and will then share, to give all from your true heart,
Tell all who want to listen, that we are 'one' and do not part.

Yes 'one' in both all time, and for each and every dimension,
And revealed then is my love, it's for all and not just 'Heaven'.
The peace, the Love and Light, that is forever there contained,
Free then are you all, from despair or hate and pain.

So now it is your moment, to truly see the light,
That lies around you all, each day and every night.
Just make now a real wish, for all that's said to be so true,
In my light I do so love you, so don't feel down or sad or blue.

Amen.

LESSON 48

PARALLEL LINES

A s you sit together becoming one with love from the Son, you'll grow and continue to learn as the 'one'. You are residing in the physical and yet you are also within and upon many dimensions, both receiving and sending parallel lines of communication and love.

Nothing is separated and nothing is divided, yet you could also be described as being a fragment of love and light, too. "How can this be?" so many ask. Perhaps the question is the answer itself. "How can *it* be so?" Again, it appears inevitable that the devotee, disciple or the inquirer from within will ask the how, why and the wherefore.

The reply is to just 'be', feel and know that in the recognition of being part of, and being whole, will be unified. This is a justification in the truth and the desire for personal growth and understanding of the light and the love that you are. This is your very existence and of all things imaginable.

Understand lines of communication and truth come in many ways and forms and often people will think that they are from 'out there'. In taking this conception too far it can be misunderstood and this is because 'out there' is also within one (self) and vice versa.

Everything is whole and yet co-exists on the planes of dimension and vibration, of time and space, is separate and yet complete. There is division, but nothing is diverse for love and light is, was and always will be the same, it is Universal forever.

The gifts that many of you share in a variety of different means in the transference from the source are indeed very special. No one particular method of communication is more special or is treated any differently, and it is important one does not believe that this is the case. This can be hard to accept for your hearts often request this or that, the chance to truly see or feel or understand in the way that another does.

You can compare this with your earthly senses. For example, would a blind person wish they were deaf so that they could see? Would someone who cannot touch, wish that they could not taste instead? The scenarios that can be considered are often viewed just like these, where you reside.

Also, the gifts that you each develop are for your own individual growth and purpose. No one is better than another. On the outside someone may appear more holy, gentler and more caring, yet it can sometimes be deceptive. It is the truth in and from the heart that counts and what is shown may not always be as important as it appears to be.

Returning to the example earlier, would the healer beg to truly 'see'? Does the channel yearn to express in other ways? Remember each step, each learning process is for the moment, so move forward and grow with these gifts by learning to appreciate them and sharing, which can only enhance what you are receiving and giving from your hearts. Again, no one is better than another, for in truth you are all equal.

It must be said that you all have these gifts, every one of you. Inside, you are all the same, made from love to give, share and expand. It is only on the outside that you seem different, and it is only the outside perception that you each have, that separates and causes the divisions in your societies, countries, and world.

The very core of each and every Soul is the same and in every being, galaxy, and in all beings of light, only perception of the exterior is different. It is this, and the combination of a Soul's growth and comprehension of its existence that creates the individuality and the character which comes across as unique and so diverse from each other.

If everyone was the same on the outside (the physical presence and body), then what has been given to you (the individual) to sample and grow in the many complex ways would be lost. Nothing can erase the freedom and individuality of the Soul deep within, so on the outside it may seem to be denied, but again this is the person's surroundings that give this impression.

There are external influences that seem to restrict and yet within the Soul there are no barriers or lock and key. This is why the planes of dimension and existence can be accessed through these gifts that I have given to each of you, yes, every single one of you.

Know that I am the truth and the light beyond comprehension that can change this. Do not fear what is said, but understand and comprehend these parallel lines of vibration and resonance that is you and your very being and all that surrounds both 'within' and 'out'.

So, does one crave for truth? Does the desire to bask in the light overwhelm the individual? Please do not let it. That said, it is very important, for balance and equalization are vital. Many know and remind others of phrases like 'as above, so below' and 'you can only learn to the level that you have reached', as well as 'too much, too soon' and 'do not run before you can walk'.

You, like children of the physical, only need to understand that at the right time in your life, truth is given. You can and must express free-will in love and peace, yet you must also balance your physical world with the higher vibrations that you seek.

Everything is compatible and everything is interlinked, with destiny, karma and life. Humankind globally must recognise this and release their fears; those of under-achievement, of failure and their fear of death of the physical.

Consider that your Soul is Universal and the Universe is your Soul. Confused? Do not be, for what makes you and your Soul, makes the Universe and vice versa. Your Soul is love, your life is love and every ingredient, atom, cell, structure and infrastructure and level of vibration is 'one'. All are whole; for you are all complete and have everything you could ever possibly need and seek within yourself.

So, if you cannot see with your physical eyes, does it mean you cannot truly witness the truth? If you have no ears, can you not hear? If you have a broken heart can you not love? Only fear and false manifestation can misconstrue this, for I have said before that you have all the gifts that you could ever ask for, so you must learn to trust in the Love and Light so that you can truly soar and take flight.

Decisions are always; always yours (the individual's) and no one, or nothing can ever take these away from you. Accept or deny thy truth or even cast it aside if you wish to. Understand the power of my Love and Light and that nothing can prevent you from your growth but yourself, your self-denial, your own boundaries and barriers that you make.

In time of pain or anguish, please do not despair and cast out, say or express that you do not care as this will compound what you may be trying to release, on a much deeper or karmic level. Remember that those in perilous situations should not give up hope and also should not just accept the situation as fate either. This is often very difficult to both comprehend and accept this entwined scenario.

I ask you now to imagine a hostage, separated from family and loved ones, which is a situation that manifests many times across the earth. Is this 'experience', this learning process, for the hostage, their family or for those that seem in control; the captors. Recognize that they have no real control.

A situation may be like this for many reasons and far beyond the control of those who feel that they can influence and misshapen free-will. Universal law is holy, it is love and experience and, however painful, may be overcome with trust and faith, so look forward to the light.

Yes, look forward to the light and in any situation it will turn out right, for the meaning of these things will become clearer as the heart becomes purer.

Love always prevails even in the most desperate situations. It can never be diminished, erased or forgotten if it is true and is in and from the heart of your Soul. Always understand this. For now, rest this pen and take flight. Your heart is open to the truth, always. Amen

LESSON 49

'GUILT... (OR SHAME)'?

I am with you always and have waited for you to pick up the pen. Please, do not think that you have put me about or troubled me in terms of time or my patience. These are trivial to me as I already know precisely when, where, what, and the why of all things.

So, as you write the title of this lesson or passage, what was your initial reaction? Did you or does anyone ever feel any guilt or shame in their lives? Again, you do not need to reply David, as I already know your heart and Soul, just as I know you all, yes, every being and every Soul throughout Creation.

The title is especially important at this stage for the collection of this book. Its purpose is to bring to the forefront of every mind and heart who reads this, specific thoughts and feelings of their own lives and surroundings and also those who exist far away.

Many, many feel that I am, or will be, angry or annoyed with them, but by now every Soul will know that this is not and never will be the case. Perhaps this very thought is just the reflection of what one actually thinks of within their self?

I do not judge anyone of you and all must follow this example. I understand that this is not always easy when you're faced with provocation, persecution, threats or stress that often materialise within the cocoon of general living.

Still, for any individual or group to move forward in love and truth, difficulties must be overcome. The problems you each find are in thinking that this occurs with some sort of inevitability, in that you feel it is your own fault. However, because the world is uniquely linked in a vast amount of ways, this is an incorrect viewpoint.

I see what occurs in and on the 'Earth plane' and how global views either affect you all in positive or negative ways. Nearly all events, ranging from your current world financial crisis to so called 'natural' disasters seem to grip and squeeze you all, which seem to shake you to the core.

The problem with many governments, and those people in power, is that they still think and believe in their own importance, feeling separate and imposing their control over someone or something. Until the world comes to terms with the concept and essence of being 'whole', negative traits will always come to the forefront and pick-away at the love and light and the good that many do.

In times of struggle, I feel many a heart whose pleas and cries ring out and pierce me like a dagger. Of course this is an expression of speech only, for I am beyond all such things. What I say to you is that your emotions are magnified tenfold when what you are feeling, whether it is in pain or joy of body, mind or Soul is released in truth. What can filter or fade away is the false anxiety in the loss of material possessions and anything else that belongs in the impermanent world.

Within the current economic climate, people across the globe shout or scream that the value of their shares have decreased or fallen sharply, which sends them into a blind panic. So too, the value of people's homes may drop by thousands of pounds, dollars, euros or whatever the currency of the country you reside in.

Fear, or 'false' fear, grips nation after nation as one country's wealth decreases and, just like a set of dominoes, one falls down after the other. Panic sets in, being stirred and raised by media speculation and so forth. People talk of their assets dwindling and yet they still live in a house, they have food on the table and shoes on their feet.

When the eyes of the Soul, heart and mind are fully open as one, you will see through these events and then look upon the truth. When you see your neighbour as part of you, you will then feel the truth. When you outstretch your hand to help a stranger, you will know the truth.

As people discuss the price of oil and fuel for their cars and homes, little thought is given for the host and the 'giver' of such things. Mother Earth is where your physical resides and she provides you with all that your body needs to function. You grow crops which nourish all living things and the rain falls to quench your thirst. The Earth is so beautiful and amazing, and yet it is only in the last few years that people are taking notice of her vulnerability and condition.

I hear the words, 'these uncertain times' millions of times a day from those that have strayed. What can any one person do about it? How can they help protect the Earth and those upon it? These are the more important questions.

The thoughts of one can help to change the many. By tending to one's own garden (your character and personality) and living and nurturing true human values, then the seeds of love will sprout further a field.

Currently you could picture acres and acres of barren soil or fields of weeds that, through perseverance and understanding of your fellow man's needs, will become full of light and spiritual growth. Then, like a patchwork quilt they will be sown together to form a collective layer of hope and peace that will cover the earth in a blanket of love.

I Am I: The In-Dweller of Your Heart

So I now state, in returning to the beginning of this lesson, do you feel any guilt or shame? Have you been true to yourself this day? Could you have helped another Soul in your society today? Did the opportunity pass you by? Does this now make you want to weep and cry?

One great factor that you can foster in your life is contentment. If you have food in your stomach, do you think of those who hunger? If your throat is moist or wet from water, do you sense or feel for those who thirst? When you have friends who you can call upon to help you in your hour of need, is a thought spared for those who are lonely, lost or sad? Try to be content in the areas of your life that truly matter.

Do not ever be afraid or worry in doom or gloom. Your hearts can bask in the glory of the Son each and every day and the Sun will also shine and rain will fall somewhere upon the world. This is promised and hence it is so important the Earth's resources are shared fairly, evenly, with care and compassion.

One day, if you believe, if you hope and pray, and if all beings are true to themselves, this will happen. Do not sink into yourself, so that your light lies in shadow. You are a living flame and I urge you to move forward, even just one small step at a time to shine more brightly.

Your illumination will make others bask in a feeling of warmth and serenity and, like a link in a chain, all Souls will realise they are connected together in an unbroken cord of love. Some will state though, that, like any chain, it is only as strong as the weakest link, but I recommend you to forget these chains of the impermanent world that they think they now compare.

You are me, as I am you and as such, any so-called fragment, part, or any child of light, is all power and all strength that can be deemed to exist. Nothing, absolutely nothing, can ever break my bond to you. You are all the very fabric of my own heart and existence.

I urge and implore you all to grow and fulfil your destiny. Release any guilt or shame trailing behind you right now in your lives. Help the love that lies beside, or near you, or on the other side of the world by being true and kind in all you do, think and pray.

You can change the way all the nations of your world act and react with each other if you believe in yourself and each other. For if you do, then you also believe in me. Remember, you are never alone, for I am with you always and forever. Amen.

LESSON 50

WAR AND PEACE, LOVE AND HATE

Welcome. Let me start this lesson, this transcript, this guidance and education by explaining that I do not condemn or condone thought, words and deeds on your physical level. All action and therefore its result, you (and you all) bring to bear yourselves. It has been and always will be this way.

As this is the case, it is your own life and with it the ability to enhance or degenerate life and all the things around you that is displayed upon minds, bodies or spirits. As stated before, these can be deemed as separate elements of the 'I', but in essence they are one as they make you complete. So, now let us begin with War and Peace.

Since human beings roamed the earth, before speech even began, man, woman, and child could either live in harmony or in conflict. Throughout history too, this was the same within families, groups, gatherings and in villages, towns, cities, and countries the world over.

Even today, with all your technology and experience, all people have the same choices as back then. In this respect, time has made no difference. So, how does war start? Who starts it? Why does conflict come to bear?

Simple thoughts could take you back to easier times of childhood and innocence to explain many things, for even as a child, one could display aspects of a character that would usually remain hidden. People would often cry or argue a point of view such as "that's mine!" or "I'm not sharing it"! Now, some who read these lines may start to accuse me of over-simplicity or have all sorts of thoughts or feelings themselves they wish to convey on these matters. This is good, for we all need to rethink about who, what and why we exist and more importantly co-exist amongst all sorts of 'life'.

All truth is simple and I am not going to baffle or make people feel as if they have a complex or any lack of understanding. You only need an understanding that requires one to unblock the past which leads to your 'present,' and you're present which leads to your 'future'.

War occurs when two minds, or rather two hearts, do not meet or share in truth of what they are. This then splinters into greed, jealousy, pride, hate, and all thoughts of power over another. These are but needles that pierce and blind true sight, casting eyes into shadow, doom and gloom.

People cry out to me from the depths of despair, "Why God do you let this happen? How could you take them away from me? When did you

156

stop caring for us?" All these I hear, see, sense, and feel with all that I am. Nothing is lost or diluted, whether in joy or pain, for I am you and you are me. So, why should he or she suffer? Why should this or that country be war torn or ravaged by such things?

Do you wish to know? More importantly are you ready to know? Time and time again we revert to the past and 'karma', cause and effect, balance and imbalance, and light and darkness. All these answers you know already.

Finite details are not required, for you do not need me to recite examples of conflict after conflict, war after war throughout your history. What is more important now is for every individual to open heart and Soul to truth, love and light.

Peace comes to all those who do not desire anyone or anything. Those that dilute and dissolve their ego find inner peace more quickly, and then they find their true self. Finding their true self brings illumination and recognition of their Divinity and of me. Once you recognise this, understanding becomes easier, life becomes fulfilling and you can blossom into the Soul and light that you were meant to be.

One can ask of me, 'I want peace, let there be peace, bring peace to…..' etcetera, but what is it that is actually requested and wished for? Is it for comfort, joy and stillness? Is it for others to find help, shelter, protection, food, or water? Peace encompasses all things for, when nothing is required, then peace reigns.

When will this happen? First you need to all find the peace within yourself, and then by linking with your neighbour, family, friends, or even a stranger, the chains of love are formed.

Love is the strongest force imaginable. As discussed before, true love cannot be broken by time or distance. Memories can fade but the imprint upon your heart and Soul is eternal. This is why no matter what incarnation you actually find yourself in, you can find, know, and live eternally within me.

Answers that many seek within your lives are found within the question you ask, yet you already know. The to and fro is the inner battle that each individual embarks upon. Your feelings and intuition are the gauges that swing from truth and love via illusion and hate. Consequently, every one of you constantly wages your own inner war to find peace. The hate that can ooze from every cell of the body is but the negativity and confusion that must be erased. Hate brings anguish, anguish leads to fear, fear leads to stress, and stress is 'disease' (ill at ease) and death of the body.

Hate is blindness to another's love and joy. It is also a reflection that one can see in a mirror at a funfair. It distorts and contorts the true image of light itself. It detracts you away from the rays of the Sun that beam the radiance both within and out.

Today, this minute of this hour, you can change. You can make a difference to your own life, Soul and destiny. From the alterations you make, you can effect and cast light beyond; far beyond your heart and the walls of your home, wherever that may be.

Do not ever despair or fear any situation. I am not saying for anyone to be ruthless or careless in any 'action' that they take, but rather request that you find your direction in the truth. I am nearer than near and I will never leave you. Through your worst 'pain' or greatest joy, I am with and within you. Believe me like I always believe in you. We are 'one' forever, and I will lead you into bliss. Amen.

LESSON 51

HAPPINESS

Happiness… is it only for the few, for some other or is it just for you? Many people of all ages and in all walks of life strive in the so called 'pursuit' of some kind of elusive pleasure. It does not matter whether you are old and grey or even an infant opening its eyes from re-birth. This is because 'inbuilt' inside of you, is the feeling of a burning 'ill fated' desire that both haunts and casts its shadow over almost every thought flashing through your mind and to the daily acts of work, rest, and play.

This incorrect notion all stems from desire of this or that, a craving from anything and to anything. It could be material, emotional, physical but none the less the false and sometimes dangerous illusion comes first and foremost from the mind.

So, looking deeper into this scenario, a child craves comfort, having the need to feel warm, to be fed and to try and test all that is around them. A continual want, want, want takes hold for almost anything. Ask any parent who carries their kin through any toy or sweet shop. Some will give in, "I've got this because it made them happy", but this is a temporary solution that will never fulfil their one true need.

As man grows and matures through adolescence, adulthood, parenthood and retirement, sooner or later 'he' is tested by his own feelings of need. Again, this is delusion. Please do not take offence, for there is absolutely nothing wrong in striving to achieve personal goals and ambitions. Subsequently, if from your labour and hard work, fruits are born and enter your domain, then these can be 'just rewards'. There is nothing wrong with that at all.

It is when the attachments of such takes hold of the heart which then leads to feelings of inadequacy, disharmony and the person becomes discontent. People look at their spouses, homes, cars, neighbours, and relatives, etcetera and can often feel that they wish they had made different choices. 'Not satisfied with their lot' springs to mind.

Before the reader feels that this lesson or message sounds like a lecture or a telling off, please do not feel this way. All words, pictures and feelings are given to reflect and share the truth. If it were not so, you would have placed this book, these pages of text to one side by now.

I reiterate such things only to point out the necessary striving that

159

seems deep set in the psyche of man. All Souls need only one goal and that is to return to your true home and place of residence which is my heart. This is where you will find your true happiness and pure bliss. It cannot ever be found in the latest gadget or new car, home or partner. All 'Earth plane' connections that are not Soul to Soul or heart to heart dissipate and fade, true happiness does not.

A comparison of false happiness that is sought so frequently is like a stone tossed into a clear pool of water. It will cause concentric rings to ripple out. At first they're seen very clearly but then they will disappear from view as if it never happened at all.

The stone, the weight of a false hope, has sunk into the depths of your heart. In contrast for example, when two people are in love they will remember their first kiss, the first time they held hands and even where, when, and what time it was then they first met!

So, you could say that love is happiness and happiness is love. However, think about the time when you remember being in love or recall the deepest, strongest bond you have for a person, pet, place, or even for something that you had 'seen'. If you could multiply this by infinity then this is bliss and true peace and contentment.

So how can you be happy? Is it when you have the brand new car? Are you fulfilled when you get that promotion or new home, pet or partner? No, because all are impermanent and form attachment. However, to be free I say you do not need to give up these things but to change the importance and priority of such within your lives.

I request that you simply trust in yourself and in me. Have strength and conviction in your faith and hope in all you do. Have confidence in your ability to overcome hardship and transgressions. Make no doubt about it, in time, overcoming and changing your state of mind that tricks and beholds you, you will see and become 'lighter' in all you say and do.

Every day and every night you can make a difference to your own life and in those of who you meet. Your vibration level will increase and you will resonate and send love that is within you to those close by and also to all those who touch your heart both near and afar.

Sceptics will say to you that happiness is a state of mind, yet I explain that your true happiness lies outside of your mind. It is without mind, for there you do not need to think, or conjure up images, or feelings, of desire.

People have known the words, "I want happiness" and "I want peace" and, as explained before, if you take away the 'I' (which relates to ego) and take away the 'want' (the desire) you are left with the goal and the truth.

I say to you, push open the prison bars that captivate the mind. Indeed, the door was already open when you thought you had needed a new key. So, open your heart and make the mind free. Guide it from the cell and those false barriers that you yourself erected. Nothing can stop you, nothing can hurt you, for you are I and I am you. This alone will bring you home to be eternally happy, and happily 'eternal'. Be at peace and rest, God bless. Amen.

LESSON 52

THE CHOICE

Welcome to you and all of the light, life and love. As you sit you have wondered of the title of his lesson. In fact, you have pondered upon it for many days now, thinking and hoping for what you would call, 'something special'.

I know your feelings of gratitude and humbleness that shine from your heart, and also your hope for the illumination of insight, wisdom and knowledge. Indeed, these can all be deemed special, but for whom does it apply to?

One Soul who needs just one sentence of this book may feel bewildered and confused. Another, like a lightning bolt from the sky, may find inspiration to carry on, to then fulfil his or her goal in life, whatever that may be.

Throughout the times that you have been cognisant of me (and my voice that echoes through your heart and mind), have your feelings changed at all? I could explain and suggest they have for you have perused and carried on your work of service willingly and eagerly. If this was not the case then this book that is being collated would never have reached page 2.

Many Souls will look to these pages for many reasons, including their inquisitiveness, personal growth, understanding, hope, or even a yearning for the feeling that life has a purpose, a reason for living.

The list is endless and yet all these are the same, for ultimately everything is for, towards, to or from love. Every aspect and facet of life and light is for one purpose. Nothing can alter it; nothing can deceive it or delay its outcome.

Only an individual can challenge themselves where their destiny is concerned. Only the Soul will comprehend its actions, it's freewill to adjust to the path of righteousness or self-denial.

Before one states that I may be heavy-handed in my expressions, one has to realise that every lesson in this book was explained and shared for a reason, at a particular point and for each and every season.

We have spoken many times over the years about 'time' and its relevance upon the 'Earth plane'. Likewise, each lesson falls upon its appropriate page and space when required to do so.

For those that pick up this book, you may start at Lesson 1 and follow the course of events or you may choose any particular Lesson at random.

I Am I: The In-Dweller of Your Heart

Whatever takes place is because you need it.

Throughout your lives, it is the same principle; everything has its purpose and its reason for being. Know that a need or desire is never dismissed, but the seeds are planted through your own efforts. Recognition is gained and situations occur when they are meant to, not when you want them to.

Ultimately, any path that is chosen, any event that occurs to you or any so-called positive or negative situation is down to the result being for your higher good, karma and Soul.

Do not concern yourself or box yourself in with worries or doubts. These will slow you down, preventing you from picking up pace towards your self-realisation. It is enough to simply 'be' in thought, word and deed.

Do not pretend to be someone who you are not. Do not feel that you have to justify your existence to anyone else or anything on any place or dimension. You are who you are and everything around you is temporary and of the mind's illusion.

You think of yourself as a body with a Soul or even vice versa. You also feel that your mind dictates to you and you can be agitated by what can be viewed as minor irritations or inconveniences.

Know that you are as 'I am'. You are Light and Love; a resonance of Divinity. It is you and only you that can comprehend your own internal brilliance. It cannot be seen by a mirror, for that reflection is false, fleeting and impermanent for the impermanent world.

You each have a choice. You can make it right this second, or you could delay or, perhaps, even deny it altogether. Suddenly thoughts flash across the brain and mind, the impulses and signals swirling about causing you to think, feel, and wonder what it might be.

It doesn't matter where you are upon your quest, search and journey (or whatever level you or anyone else believes you're on), do you progress, standstill or continue the old ways of living and being?

This day can be a new beginning and deemed a start of something brilliant that changes your life and those around you forever. Each day forthwith can be lived as if it was your last, with meaning, justification and of hope and glory. The light and the love that emanates from you and the kindness and peace that pours from your heart are limited only by yourself.

You can light the beacon of joy and hope by reigniting the spark of your Soul's flame. You will then radiate and bloom with serenity and splendour, majestic in both simplicity and in grace. By your very nature you will nurture those who will draw close to you, captivating them with a smile and guiding them with an open hand. All of this you can 'realise' and also be upon your path and choice that remains to be seen.

I Am I: The In-Dweller of Your Heart

It is important that you remember and that no one sees this as a test, which I decree or have set. As I am you and you are me, this was in place and always has been, for there was no beginning and there shall be no end.

This choice is only current because of the way that all Souls have manifested and grown through time and experience, through freewill and Karma, with a false sense of separation and illusion when there is none. You are all 'one'. Nothing, absolutely nothing, can alter or change this fact and truth.

No matter where you reside or what religion you have followed or practiced, find its truth and its strength. I will never ask you to stop or deny your earthly heritage or practices. You only need to walk the path of honesty and integrity and share your love.

If you do, then no persuasion or a delusion or twist of fate can make you hurt anyone or anything. It is man, and man alone, who misconstrues or diverges from this path to want to govern or hold power over another person or land.

In no text or wisdom of heart has hate or anger ever been decreed to do these things. If these occur, it is then your freewill to uphold your true beliefs. Do not fear for I am with you, always in all ways.

This lesson is drawing to a close, David. Your guides will conclude with you upon the final words of the book and cover. You have grown, as have those friends who have shared your readings with open hearts and Souls.

Do not concern yourself or worry over 'if and where' this work is received. That has never been your concern or priority and need ever be. Trust in me as I have placed my trust in you all.

The world (Earth) is a beautiful place, often cast in shadow and gloom of desperation and hate. Each Soul can be the light expressed in eternal truth. Billions of you reside there, temporarily. Honour yourselves by honouring each other. Live with human values and right conduct that you are bestowed with, both within and out.

See with heart, mind, and Soul as one, to clearly view the path ahead that needs perseverance, fortitude and endurance by all. Remember to love the things that you think cannot think. Wrap your arms around those who are less fortunate on the earthly road that you tread.

Feel, sense, and know me in the grass, flowers, trees, rivers, seas, mountains, sky, fire, earth and the space beyond. *Realise* me in the stillness within yourself. Here I reside with you for you to understand and grow.

I will never leave you and always love you. Your heart is my heart and your life can be an expression of the Divinity that is truly you. Be at peace and fulfil your destiny. Your dreams are my dreams and I will help you fulfil them all. We are 'one', always and forever. Amen.

PS. David, you will decide to continue in this vein with your writing until new avenues and routes are appropriate. The next book – **I am I: The In-Dweller of your Heart (Part 2)** will be ready and waiting when it is needed.

CONCLUSION –
FROM THE CONNECTION (Part 1)

GOD'S LOVE

Unique, brilliant, majestic, all powerful and healing, it is all and the all is love. Reflect upon this statement and let it nourish the core of yourself and your 'Self'.

You yearn and contemplate, perhaps worrying and dreading your life and life's tasks that you yourself have set (or have been laid down for you), but we say, just 'be'.

There is no commandment, instruction or rule book for you to digest, read or act upon. If you simply know yourself, your 'Self' and Soul, then all will work out just right each and every day and night.

Deem that the connection is to, from, up, down, behind, in front, sideways, within, and out as every route leads to God's love. Everywhere, yes in all places, and in all beings, is the love which was not born, but given freely to all Creation.

Realise that the sweetest smell and fragrance, the lightest touch, the brightest and most warm sun (and Son), the freshest breeze, the bluest sky, the highest and most low vibration and energy are all God's love, which is within and is everything. Therefore rejoice, bask, feel, and truly be this love.

Acknowledge and be proud to have found and walk his love through the treadmill of life. Up the highest hills and your downward slopes, through your believed good and bad times, just follow, guide and share love that is free for you all.

As you well know, a beating heart of the physical pumps its blood to all the organs of the body so you are able to live the way you do. While this is so, God's heart also 'beats' the purest love to sustain and help you to grow and know the truth of whom, what and why you are.

Hence, to feel God's love and then acknowledge it, leads to understanding and the experience required for both the individual and group Soul journeys. The emphasis is plain and simple and is not complicated. '

The best things in life are free', this is truth, wisdom, and these words can be a springboard to more joy and happiness that God's love contains, if only more of you believed in love. It is unrivalled, has no comparison and

I Am I: The In-Dweller of Your Heart

no equal. There is no division, it is 'all' and all is love.

A flower and a tree are all born from just one seed,
And the rays of the true Sun are born out from a deep need.
So you bathe and are then engulfed, in peace and also love,
His power and his grace, come from within and up above.

It is right and it is now, and it is by day and then by night,
So discover and accept freely, and freely give out what is right.
No holding back of what are both, the within and the without,
No laying still, a life of love, of which there is no doubt.

From roof tops or high mountains, those do seem to touch the sky,
No need to ever wonder, or cry out asking 'Why?'
For you all have the gift, and the 'present' from his heart,
And 'one' forever is his promise… to never, ever part.

Amen.

CONCLUSION-
FROM THE CONNECTION (Part 2)

GO IN PEACE AND WITH FORGIVENESS

In one hand man has a gun and in the other an open heart. With one thought he can break it, pierce it clean through, or he can mend it with kindness, compassion, and love.

Throughout the ages, there has been a power-struggle within the body, mind, and Soul. This innate struggle manifests itself deep in the core of the 'Self' and it surfaces on many planes of time and dimension.

The effect of the so-called good and bad, light and dark, love and hate, and so forth can be felt by the individual as well as the masses, both far and wide. Each and every one of the 'billions' are connected by the light and therefore each and every action has a reaction and recoil, an effect which can transform or digest the cause.

Every thought, word and deed that is manifested has a minute or massive effect upon others and the world around and also within you. How does one perceive it? Can one control it? Do you judge it? All are questions with numerous answers. Simplicity is *always* the key.

If everything that is done by every Soul is with peace and compassion, then there is no worry, anxiety or concern. How can this be acted out by the billions, the governments and the Nations? The answer is 'easily and freely'; it only needs to be tried. There is no magical potion or formula to follow, other than the heart itself.

In your impermanent world today, in the climate of greed, envy, and desire, it can be so difficult because your mind tells you it is so. It is in new ways of believing, being, and acting whom and what you are, that brings change. It is within this understanding that all (if they wish to) must alter their 'self'.

Each and everyday contains the opportunities to alter (for the better) both within and out. Do not judge others, but be true to yourself, for all good deeds, actions, and reactions will spread and be seen by others with both physical and spiritual eyes.

Do not look, for rewards or of what is yours or mine. Simply have an open heart and Soul and let your light shine like a beacon, attracting and sending out wave after wave of vibration energy with love, peace and forgiveness.

I Am I: The In-Dweller of Your Heart

Please do not be hard upon yourselves when you are weak, but acknowledge the fact that you have recognised it as such and move on, gaining strength in fortitude and perseverance. Others will see this new strength and be inspired and act according to their own heart and mind's perception.

You are never alone as God is light, Spirit, and love, and both the high and low, the in and out, time and no time, as well as space and no space. Indeed, all things are sent and received by God. They are seen or unseen, heard or unheard, perceived or ignored, accepted or denied, loved or unloved, touched or untouched, and sensed or not sensed.

In the Spirit world, and in all dimensions, all we ask, hope, and pray for is the truth, love, and light. For all things are here and here 'within', lies all things.

Remember who and what you really are and, by experiencing and living it in the physical, it will be mirrored back and forth both within and without your Soul. Being true to both yourself and others is all anyone can ask of you. If all can follow the love within their hearts then everyone will forgive and find peace.

Do not try to find the differences between these last few words above as some will say forgiveness and peace are separate, two unrelated things, yet they are not. They are entwined, encompassed like a pearl in a shell. It is when the hardened shell of hate opens, by the action of forgiveness, that truth, beauty, and the love of peace is made known to those that reveal and share it, as well as for those who receive it.

This truth is for everyone but those who acknowledge it all, also 'will' it to happen. Be 'still' in the knowingness of this love and light. Try to open the outer casing of your own heart and expose the beauty of the completeness 'within'. Let peace shine eternally from inside your heart's centre and very Soul. Let this be the truth and so fulfil your one true goal.

Finally, thank you for writing and conveying these precious words, David, from, to and beyond the heart. Until next time you sit and become 'still', love and light within the Spirit realms and dimensions around you will be waiting. Your friends and 'family' who are from far and wide and through space and time, *will* return on the wave and tide of love. God Bless you all. Amen.

FURTHER READING

You will find your own guidance and inspiration every day, week, month or year as nothing in life is ever by 'chance'. Each Lesson will simply be the most appropriate for your needs at that time, helping you to find inner peace and balance as well as your own spiritual education, growth and understanding. Here is a selection of my favourite books / authors and which I hope you will enjoy reading.

Sai Baba Gita-
The Way to Self Realization and Liberation in this age.
By Al Drucker
ISBN 0-9638449-0-3

Conversations with God
By Neale Donald Walsh
Book 1 - ISBN 0-340-69325-8
Book 2 - ISBN 0-340-76544-5
Book 3 - ISBN 0-340-76545-3

The Message of a Master
By John McDonald
ISBN 0-931432-95-2

The Celestine Prophecy- An Adventure
By James Redfield
ISBN 0-533-40902-6

Anastasia- The Ringing Cedar series -Book 1
By Vladimir Megre
ISBN 978-0-9801812-0-3

A Course in Miracles
By The Foundation for Inner Peace
ISBN 0-670-86975-9

The Winds of Change
By Stephanie J. King
ISBN 9780954242169

The Day my life changed
By Carmel Reilly
ISBN 978-1-84509-420-1

Confessions of a Pilgrim
Bu Paulo Coelho
ISBN 0-7225-3293-8

A Mind of your Own
By Betty Shine
ISBN 0-00-255894-7

Angel Inspiration
By Diana Cooper
ISBN 0-340-73323-3

Chicken Soup for the Soul
By Jack Confield and Mark Victor Hansen
ISBN 0-09185-428-8

The Complete Book of Dreams
By Edwin Raphael
ISBN 0-572-01714-6

The Bible Code
By Michael Drosnin
ISBN 0-297-82994-7

About the Author

DAVID KNIGHT was born into his current physical embodiment in 1964. He is married to Caroline and they live with their adopted cats Toby, Treacle, Spiky and Missy in Northamptonshire in the UK. In growing up he describes himself as a Mr. Average or like a 'Joe Bloggs'. Whilst earning a living in various types of work, (this ranged from HM Forces, Financial Services, a Care Assistant and self-employment), his search for fulfilment changed from the exterior and without to the interior and within.

Spiritual education gained a greater momentum and at the age of 21 a more urgent sense of dedication as well as a new realization had set in. New evidence of and from God, were soon revealed through his life experiences. With the aid of Spirit guides and beings from the ethereal planes, the foundations were laid for all who wished to develop and experience their Hearts flame of love and light and to embark upon a unique opportunity for all Soul's in this lifetime.

Made in the USA
Charleston, SC
24 November 2011